KOREMATSU *v.*
THE UNITED STATES

ABDO
Publishing Company

KOREMATSU *v.*
THE UNITED STATES

WORLD WAR II JAPANESE-AMERICAN INTERNMENT CAMPS

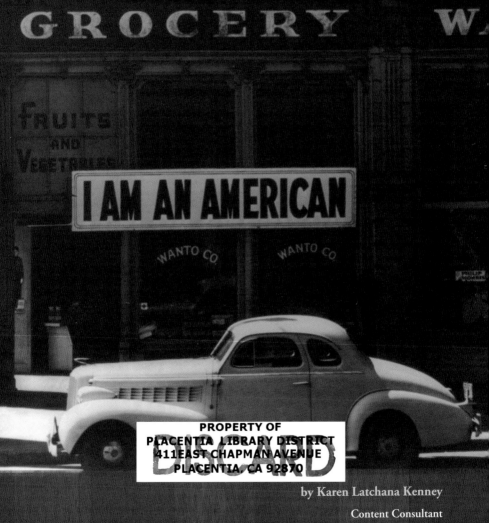

GROCERY

W

FRUITS AND VEGETABLES

I AM AN AMERICAN

WANTO CO.

WANTO CO.

by Karen Latchana Kenney

Content Consultant
Richard D. Friedman
Alene and Allan F. Smith Professor of Law
University of Michigan Law School

CREDITS

Published by ABDO Publishing Company, PO Box 398166, Minneapolis, MN 55439. Copyright © 2013 by Abdo Consulting Group, Inc. International copyrights reserved in all countries. No part of this book may be reproduced in any form without written permission from the publisher. The Essential Library™ is a trademark and logo of ABDO Publishing Company.

Printed in the United States of America,
North Mankato, Minnesota
042012
092012

Editor: Melissa York
Series Designer: Emily Love
Special thanks to Richard Friedman, Content Consultant for chapters 1–10.

Library of Congress Cataloging-in-Publication Data
Kenney, Karen Latchana.
  Korematsu v. the United States : World War II Japanese-American internment camps / by Karen Latchana Kenney ; content consultant Richard D. Friedman.
    p. cm. -- (Landmark Supreme Court cases)
  Includes bibliographical references.
  ISBN 978-1-61783-473-8
  1. Korematsu, Fred, 1919---Trials, litigation, etc.--Juvenile literature. 2. United States--Trials, litigation, etc.--Juvenile literature. 3. Japanese Americans--Evacuation and relocation, 1942-1945--Juvenile literature. 4. Trial and arbitral proceedings I. Friedman, Richard D., 1951- II. Title. III. Title: Korematsu vs. the United States. IV. Title: Korematsu versus the United States.
  KF228.K59K46 2013
  341.6'7--dc23

                              2012001277

Photo Credits
Clem Albers/National Archives, cover; Dorothea Lange/National Archives, 3, 41, 60, 67, 75; Photo courtesy of Karen Korematsu and the Korematsu Institute, 9, 29; Ansel Adams/Library of Congress, 14, 87; Bettmann/Corbis/AP Images, 23, 48, 95; Alfred T. Palmer/Library of Congress, 32; US Navy/Library of Congress, 34; Elias Goldensky/Library of Congress, 39; Red Line Editorial, 80; Harris and Ewing/Library of Congress, 107; Photo Property of Farallon Films, Permission Granted by the Korematsu Institute, 123; Paul J. Richards/AFP/Getty Images, 131; Brennan Linsley/AP Images, 135

Table of Contents

WHAT IS THE US SUPREME COURT?

The US Supreme Court, located in Washington DC, is the highest court in the United States and authorized to exist by the US Constitution. It consists of a chief justice and eight associate justices nominated by the president of the United States and approved by the US Senate. The justices are appointed to serve for life. A term of the court is from the first Monday in October to the first Monday in October the following year.

Each year, the justices are asked to consider more than 7,000 cases. They vote on which petitions they will grant. Four of the nine justices must vote in favor of granting a petition before a case moves forward. Currently, the justices decide between 100 and 150 cases per term.

The justices generally choose cases that address questions of state or federal laws or other constitutional questions they have not previously ruled on. The Supreme Court cannot simply declare a law unconstitutional; it must wait until someone appeals a lower court's ruling on the law.

HOW DOES THE APPEALS PROCESS WORK?

A case usually begins in a local court. For a case involving a federal law, this is usually a federal district court. For a case involving a state or local law, this is a local trial court.

If a defendant is found guilty in a criminal trial and believes the trial court made an error, that person may appeal the case to a higher court. The defendant, now called an appellant, files a brief that explains the error the trial court allegedly made and asks for the decision to be reversed.

An appellate court, or court of appeals, reviews the records of the lower court but does not look at other evidence or call witnesses. If the appeals court finds no errors were made, the appellant may go one step further and petition the US Supreme Court to review the case. A case ruled on in a state's highest court may be appealed to the US Supreme Court.

A Supreme Court decision is based on a majority vote. Occasionally one or more justices will abstain from a case, however, a majority vote by the remaining justices is still needed to overturn a lower-court ruling. What the US Supreme Court decides is final; there is no other court to which a person can appeal. In addition, these rulings set precedent for future rulings. Unless the circumstances are greatly changed, the Supreme Court makes rulings that are consistent with its past decisions. Only an amendment to the US Constitution can overturn a Supreme Court ruling.

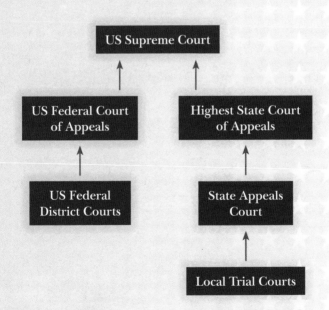

Chapter 1

An Unexpected Visitor

The guard entered Fred T. Korematsu's cell at the federal jail in San Francisco, California, and said, "Fred, you have a visitor."[1] Korematsu had no idea who could be visiting him. All of Korematsu's friends and family were enlisted in the armed services, or they had already gone to the Japanese-American assembly centers, temporary holding facilities built on racetracks, county fairgrounds, or other large spaces.

It was 1942, and the world was in the midst of war. World War II (1939–1945) raged in Europe as the Allied powers, which included Britain and France at the time, fought against the Axis powers, which included Germany, Italy, and Japan. After Japan's

Fred Korematsu's life changed completely in the 1940s.

surprising and deadly attack on the Pearl Harbor naval base in Hawaii on December 7, 1941, the United States had entered the war. Feelings toward the Japanese were growing hostile in the United States. Even Japanese Americans born on US soil were suspected of being enemies. In early 1942, Executive Order 9066 changed their lives completely. All people of Japanese ancestry, US citizens or not, who lived on the West Coast were excluded, or forced to leave their homes. They were transported to assembly centers and then internment camps where they were to live while the United States was at war. Korematsu resisted, though, and refused to

EXECUTIVE ORDERS

An executive order is a command or action issued by the US president. It is usually directed at government officials and agencies, while only indirectly affecting individuals. Generally, the president issues an executive order to direct the government how to carry out laws. Although the Constitution does not specifically state the president can issue executive orders, every president since the founding of the United States has issued at least one. These orders have wielded power over a wide range of issues: from Japanese-American internment to provisions in the health care law that was passed in 2010. Some commentators believe executive orders are used as a way to bypass the legislative process.

leave. In a later interview Korematsu recalled thinking, "I am an American . . . I have nothin' to do with Japan."[2] Korematsu's actions, which were a violation of the executive order, resulted in his arrest on May 30, 1942.

The night the guard told him he had a visitor, Korematsu did not know who it could be. But he went to the jail's visitor room anyway. Waiting for him was a young man in a gray suit. He introduced himself: "I'm Ernest Besig, and I'm an attorney. . . . I belong to the [American Civil Liberties Union]. Is there anybody helping you on your case?"[3]

Besig, who was the executive director of the American Civil Liberties Union of Northern California (ACLU-NC) at the time, had read about Korematsu's arrest in a local newspaper. It was just the kind of case that he was looking for—a US citizen of Japanese descent who refused to go to the internment camps. He believed it would make a good test case to challenge the **constitutionality** of the internment camps and the federal order—one that might even make it to the United States Supreme Court.

constitutionality—Being in accordance with a constitution.

The ACLU-NC and Besig had been watching the progression of events that led to the internment of Japanese Americans. They believed it was a clear example of US citizens being denied their constitutional rights, the kind of case typically challenged by the ACLU-NC and its national headquarters. Besig met with the Japanese American Citizen's League (JACL) to try to persuade them to oppose the exclusion and internment of Japanese Americans. But the JACL was not interested in discussing the issue. They believed that fully cooperating with the internment would prove their loyalty to the US government and its people, and they promoted this belief to the Japanese-American community. That is one reason Korematsu's case was so unusual from the beginning. Many Japanese Americans

THE AMERICAN CIVIL LIBERTIES UNION

The American Civil Liberties Union (ACLU) fights for the civil rights of Americans, even if the cause is unpopular. It was founded in 1920. Its staff and volunteer lawyers handle civil liberties cases across the country. The ACLU has been involved with many landmark cases in US history. It supported Korematsu at a time when virtually no other organization would. It has represented unpopular groups with ideals the ACLU does not necessarily agree with, such as the American Nazis, showing that the organization is an unbiased defender of civil rights. For 90 years, the ACLU has been involved with more Supreme Court cases than any other private organization.

did not protest their internment; only a few, including Korematsu, did.

In the jail's visitor's room, Korematsu could not believe his good fortune. There was a lawyer sitting in front of him, someone he had never met and did not know, who was willing to help him. Even after the newspapers had claimed Korematsu was a "Jap Spy," Besig wanted the ACLU to take his case.[4] Besig discussed wanting to turn Korematsu's case into a test case. He warned Korematsu that the road to the Supreme Court might be difficult. Korematsu later recalled that Besig said, "Whatever threats that you get . . . we'll fight it

Few Japanese protested when they were forced to uproot their lives and relocate to internment camps such as Manzanar Relocation Center in California.

together, all the way."[5] Korematsu believed Besig was the only person who could help him: no one in the Japanese-American community could help, nor would the JACL help. At that point, Korematsu knew what he wanted to do. He would allow the ACLU to represent him.

Together they would challenge not only Korematsu's arrest, but also the constitutionality of the Japanese-American internment.

Korematsu's Decision

When Korematsu refused to go to the internment camps, he made a conscious decision to break a law he felt was unfair, unjust, and **unconstitutional**. The decision was an act of civil disobedience. Korematsu purposely disobeyed a law to make a statement about its fairness. Korematsu was a US citizen who did not feel he should have to leave his home because of his ethnicity. His case pushed the Japanese-American internment issue before the courts, where it could be analyzed for its constitutionality. It raised a number of deeper issues, too. Should the law equally protect all citizens, even during wartime? Are people always entitled to **due process of law**? Is it constitutional for the government to take away the rights of people because of their ethnicity? Does ethnicity determine a person's loyalty to the United

due process of law—A basic principle in the US legal system that requires fairness in the government's dealings with people.

unconstitutional—Inconsistent with a constitution.

States? Should citizens, the **legislative branch**, or the **judicial branch** have the right to question or protest executive wartime orders? Or should those orders be accepted without question?

Korematsu's decision to disobey the law was influenced by his personal experiences with racism, and it was just the beginning of his decades-long

judicial branch—One of three branches of the federal government; it includes the nation's court system and decides if laws are constitutional.

legislative branch—One of three branches of the federal government; it includes the US Congress and makes laws.

civil rights struggle. By deciding to take his case to the Supreme Court, he was going to stand up to the government and fight for his and other Japanese Americans' civil rights. But Korematsu's struggle was not the first that had faced Japanese Americans and other Asians in the United States. A long history of injustices forged a discriminatory trend that would later lead to internment. ∼

Chapter 2

The Japanese in the United States

When Japanese immigrants began arriving on US soil in the late nineteenth century, there was already a history of anti-Asian sentiment in the United States. The first instance of discrimination in immigration laws is found in the Naturalization Act of 1790. This act established that, "any alien, being a free white person, who shall have resided [in the] United States for the term of two years, may be admitted to become a citizen thereof . . ."[1] This meant that only Caucasians, generally people of European origin, were legally allowed to **naturalize**. This law discriminated against any person who was not Caucasian. This included people of African descent, who were subjected to slavery in the United States at that time. In 1870, people of African descent were granted the right of naturalized citizenship. However, Asians were still denied this right. After the US Civil War (1861–1865), the act was interpreted to prohibit Chinese immigrants from becoming US citizens.

Although they could not become citizens, Chinese people began immigrating to the United States in increasing numbers in the mid-nineteenth century. Immigrants may remain citizens of their original country, or they may try to naturalize to their adopted country. Many Chinese immigrants settled in California and worked as railroad laborers. As the Chinese population grew, anti-Chinese sentiment also increased. Many European immigrants believed the Chinese were taking their jobs during the economic troubles of the time. In 1882, the Chinese Exclusion Act was passed. This law suspended the immigration of Chinese citizens to the United States. It was the first time a law limited the immigration of a group of people based on their ethnicity. This law was initially intended to last for ten years, but was renewed in 1892 for another ten years.

naturalize—To become a US citizen.

In 1902, it was made permanent. This ban on Chinese immigration would not be lifted until 1943, after Chinese people had been excluded from the United States for more than 60 years.

Japanese Immigration

In the late nineteenth century, Japanese immigrants began arriving in the United States. The number of Japanese immigrants, who were initially welcomed, steadily increased, and approximately 127,000 entered the United States between 1901 and 1908.[2]

Early Japanese immigrants were mostly young male laborers. Many were skilled farmers or fishermen, and they later brought their wives to the United States. They knew how to cultivate poor lands into crop-yielding

THE "YELLOW PERIL"

First aimed at Chinese immigrants, the term *yellow peril* was soon applied to Japanese immigrants. This term refers to the skin color, yellow, historically associated with Asian people. It was a metaphor for an irrational and racist fear that Asians would overpopulate the United States, taking away the jobs and wages of Caucasians. Images and articles perpetuating this fear were shown throughout the US media, from newspaper articles to cartoons to movies.

farms, and they had knowledge of soil conditions, fertilizers, and irrigation and drainage systems. Many settled in California and in Hawaii, which was annexed by the United States in 1900. These first generation immigrants are called Issei. Issei were not welcomed into US social and economic affairs, and they could not participate in politics because they could not become

GENERATIONS OF JAPANESE AMERICANS

The different generations of Japanese Americans are referred to as Issei, Nisei, and Sansei. Issei are the first generation that arrived in the United States from Japan. Many arrived not understanding English or US culture. They brought their language, customs, and traditions, and were proud of their Japanese culture, which emphasized traditional social values and community and family relationships. They typically worked as farmers. Nisei are the second generation, the first family members born in the United States. They were the first in their families to be US citizens, because of their birth. Some also were Japanese citizens under Japan's laws. They attended US schools and were encouraged to become "Americanized" by their Issei parents. Nisei knew how to speak both Japanese and English and often served as English translators for their parents. Some, called Kibei, attended school in Japan. Sansei are the third generation. Many did not learn Japanese. Sansei began to question Japanese-American treatment in the United States during the civil rights movement in the second half of the twentieth century.

US citizens. They formed isolated communities along the West Coast due to the segregated nature of society at that time.

Anti-Japanese Activism

Many Californians began viewing Japanese laborers as a threat to their economic stability, just as they had viewed Chinese laborers a few years earlier. On May 7, 1900, labor groups held an anti-Japanese protest in San Francisco. Politicians adopted anti-Japanese platforms that year also. In May 1905, 67 labor unions in San Francisco formed the Asiatic Exclusion League. This group, which would later be called the Japanese and Korean Exclusion League, had the purpose of lobbying for Japanese and Korean exclusion from the United States. The press began printing articles citing the "problem" of Japanese immigration, with headlines such as "The Japanese Invasion: The Problem of the Hour," which appeared in the *San Francisco Chronicle*. Membership in the league grew to approximately 100,000 people in 1908 and helped to solidify anti-Japanese sentiments in California.[3]

The San Francisco School Board attempted to segregate the city's schools in 1906. On December 11,

This Hollywood, California, business displayed
anti-Japanese signs in 1923.

the board issued an order that prohibited Asian children,
including Japanese, from attending white schools.
This order angered the Japanese government and put
international relations between the United States and
Japan at risk. President Theodore Roosevelt intervened
and persuaded the board to rescind its order, promising
he would negotiate limits on Japanese immigration to
the United States.

The result of these discussions was the "Gentlemen's Agreement" of 1907. Under this agreement, Japan was to stop issuing passports to Japanese laborers, only granting passports to the families of laborers already in the United States. This slowed Japanese immigration, but it did not stop the Japanese population from growing in the United States as Japanese-American children, called Nisei, were born. Nisei were automatically US citizens, as are all people born on US soil.

Anti-Japanese Laws

Starting in January 1909 and continuing after World War I, anti-Japanese bills were introduced in the California legislature. The first law to pass was the Alien Land Law of 1913. This law prohibited immigrants who were ineligible for US citizenship from owning land and limited the amount of time they could lease land to three years. While the language of the law did not specify that Asians could not own land, it was directly aimed at the Japanese population. They were the most prominent ethnic group in the state that could not become citizens. Passing this law was a public statement of the anti-Japanese sentiment in California, but it did not prevent Japanese from farming and owning land. Many Issei transferred land ownership to their children or bought land in their children's names and remained guardians of their children's property.

The 1920 Alien Land Law further restricted the right of Japanese immigrants to own or lease land:

> [The Alien Land Law] prohibited any further transfer of land to Japanese nationals, forbade them to lease land, barred any corporation in which Japanese held a majority of stock from lease or purchase of land, and prohibited immigrant parents from serving as guardians for their minor citizen children.[4]

JAPANESE-AMERICAN STEREOTYPES

Common stereotypical views of Japanese Americans during the late nineteenth to early twentieth centuries were that they would never assimilate into US culture and that they were outwardly polite but inwardly sneaky and devious. An example of this stereotype was seen through the fictional portrayal of a Japanese immigrant by Wallace Irwin, a San Francisco journalist. Irwin wrote articles under the name "Hashimura Togo" in his "Letters of a Japanese Schoolboy." Irwin's articles, published in the *New York Times* and *Good Housekeeping*, in halting English, told the story of a 35-year-old Japanese immigrant who worked as a servant, attended school, and secretly planned to use his education against the United States. The popular articles perpetuated Japanese stereotypes.

Although the guardianship provision was struck down as being unconstitutional, the law limited the land owned by Japanese Americans.

While no law had yet specifically barred Japanese immigrants from becoming US citizens—the law only stated that those of nonwhite or non-African descent were ineligible—the issue was officially decided in a 1922 Supreme Court ruling. In *Takao Ozawa v. The United States*, it was determined that Japanese immigrants could not become US citizens. A longtime Hawaiian resident, Ozawa applied for US citizenship and was denied. He **appealed** his case to the US Supreme Court. The constitutionality of the Naturalization Act, which specified race as a qualifier to become a US citizen, was not challenged. Instead, the definition of "free white person" as stated in the law was questioned. Ozawa asked the court to consider if a person of Japanese descent could fit into that racial definition. The court stated in its opinion,

The question then is: Who are comprehended within the phrase "free white persons"? . . . The

appealed—Petitioned a higher court to review the decision or proceedings of a lower court.

federal and state courts, in an almost unbroken line, have held that the words "white person" were meant to indicate only a person of what is popularly known as the Caucasian race. . . . With the conclusion reached in these several decisions we see no reason to differ.[5]

With this Supreme Court decision, which upheld the lower court decisions, it was legally defined that a Japanese immigrant was ineligible for US citizenship.

Then Japanese immigration was completely stopped. The Immigration Act of 1924 set a "national origins" quota for immigrants. This quota limited the number of immigrants from a given country based on the population census of 1890. The act also barred people of Asian descent, including the Japanese, from coming to the United States. Although the Japanese government protested, the US government upheld the law.

Korematsu's Family

In 1906, Korematsu's father emigrated from Fukuoka, Japan, to the racially charged atmosphere of San Francisco. He started a floral nursery in East Oakland, a city across the bay from San Francisco, and Korematsu's mother later left Japan to join him. Korematsu was born on January 30, 1919, one of four sons. Korematsu recalled learning about discrimination against Japanese even during his childhood:

> *I went to grammar school, junior high, and high school in East Oakland. During my free time, I helped my dad in the nursery. In school, I learned about the Constitution and the concept of equal rights. But Asian immigrants weren't treated "equally," they were recognized as foreigners and couldn't own land or apply for citizenship.*[6]

Korematsu graduated from high school in 1937 and wanted to attend college, like his brothers, but his family could not afford the tuition. Instead, he stayed to work in his family's nursery. While Korematsu lived a fairly typical teenager's life, he did encounter racism. He recalled,

> *I had to be careful wherever I went. They refused to serve me whenever I went to a restaurant. I couldn't even get a haircut. In order to go to a place where I was welcome, I had to go to Chinatown.*[7]

Korematsu and his family continued to work in their nursery. His brothers returned from college and helped out as well. It was at this time, during the late

Fred Korematsu, *third from left*, and his family

1930s, that news of the war in Europe was heard around the United States. The US government hoped to remain neutral, but that position would soon change. ∼

Chapter 3

The Attack on Pearl Harbor

By the end of the 1930s, war in Europe was beginning. Germany, led by Adolf Hitler and the Nazi Party, wanted to dominate Europe and the world. The Nazis were advancing on countries in Europe—first Austria, then Czechoslovakia, and then Poland. Hitler signed alliances with Italy and Japan to form the Axis powers. France and Britain declared war on Germany in 1939, after Germany invaded Poland, and the two countries formed the beginnings of the Allied forces. Americans followed the terrifying news on the radio and in newspapers. The United States was far from the battles occurring in Europe, but the government, as well as many Americans, worried the

United States might soon become a target. The country began preparing for war.

Defense Work

Because of the threat of war, plenty of jobs were becoming available in US defense work, such as working on naval ships. Some of Korematsu's friends were working in defense, and he decided to join them. After training as a welder, he began working on ships and eventually got a job at an Oakland shipyard. He recalled,

> I worked in Oakland for about six months, and the superintendent comes to me and says, "Fred, you've been doing a good job, so we're going to give you a

A woman works on an airplane motor, June 1942. Many women went to work because laborers were needed for manufacturing, but Japanese were excluded from these jobs.

foreman's job so you'll be working on the outside of the ship."[1]

Then one day, as Korematsu went to clock in with his time card, there was a note waiting for him. He had to report to his trade union. There, he was told he no longer had a job because he was Japanese.

Being a patriotic American, Korematsu wanted to help in the war effort in any way he could and serve his country. He went with some high school friends to join the National Guard, but it said it could not accept him. Korematsu then tried to enlist in the Coast Guard with some Caucasian friends. While his friends were accepted, Korematsu was again refused. He recalled, "They just sort of laughed and [said], 'Sorry, we can't accept you.' They didn't give me any reason."[2] Due to military policy at that time, Japanese Americans were barred from enlisting. Soon, Korematsu's enlisted friends were ordered by their commanding officers to stop associating with him.

Pearl Harbor

While Germany was occupying nations across Europe, Japan was also showing its aggression. It had invaded and captured French Indochina in Southeast Asia. To try to stop Japan's advances, the United States placed an oil embargo on the country, which limited the US oil supplied to Japan. The action further damaged US-Japanese relations, which were already poor. Japan sent

The USS *Shaw* exploded during the December 7, 1941, attack on Pearl Harbor.

diplomats to meet with US officials in Washington DC in late 1941, but at the same time, they were preparing to attack.

December 7, 1941, was a quiet Sunday morning on the island of Oahu in Hawaii. While Hawaiians were still sleeping, 183 Japanese planes approached the US naval base of Pearl Harbor. At 7:55 a.m. the bombings began as the Japanese aerial forces first attacked US warplanes on the ground—destroying almost all of them. Commander Logan C. Ramsey, after seeing a low-flying Japanese bomber, sent out the message to every ship at the base in a telegraph, stating: "Air raid on Pearl Harbor X This is not a drill."[3] Next, US battleships were bombed. The USS *Oklahoma*, USS *Nevada*, USS *Arizona*, USS *West Virginia*, USS *Utah*, and USS *California* were hit. The ships were filled with servicemen, and many were injured or killed from the explosions or became trapped as the ships sank.

A second wave of Japanese planes arrived at 8:54 a.m., and more battleships were hit, including the USS *Pennsylvania* and the USS *Downes*. At 10:00 a.m., the bombings finally stopped as Japanese aircraft returned to their aircraft carriers. They declared the mission a success. In Oahu, the injured and dying filled hospitals, overwhelming nurses and doctors. The death toll would reach close to 2,400.[4] Pearl Harbor and the US naval fleet were nearly immobilized. Out of the eight US battleships in Pearl Harbor, two were destroyed and four sank or ran aground. Many other ships were damaged or destroyed, and more than 140 airplanes were damaged beyond repair.[5]

News of the Attack

That same morning, news of the attack came over the radio as Korematsu sat in his car with his Caucasian girlfriend on a hill overlooking the Bay Area. They had been talking about going on a picnic because it was such a nice day. As they listened to the account of the attack, Korematsu fell into shock—he could not believe Japan had attacked the United States. He quickly brought his girlfriend home and went to see his parents. His family, as Korematsu recalled,

> *were all around the radio listening. . . . They weren't saying very much. My mother was crying. My father was just disgusted. All that work that my parents did to that nursery; what was going to happen?*[6]

As it had to many Japanese Americans, news of the attack brought fear and anxiety to the Korematsu family. Anti-Japanese sentiments were already strong along the West Coast. With this attack, they feared things would get worse.

Declaration of War

President Franklin D. Roosevelt heard the news by phone while having lunch with an aide in the White House. A memorandum arrived a few hours later describing the damage. On the night of December 7, Roosevelt informed his cabinet and congressional leaders that he would seek to declare war with Japan. One of the cabinet members, Agriculture Secretary Claude R. Wickard, wrote of the meeting in his diary,

The meeting broke up at about 10 o'clock. Everyone was very sober. . . . Through it all the President was calm and deliberate. I could not help but admire his clear statements of the situation. He evidently realizes the seriousness of the situation and perhaps gets much comfort out of the fact that today's action will unite the American people.[7]

> "Yesterday, December 7, 1941—a date which will live in infamy—the United States of America was suddenly and deliberately attacked by naval and air forces of the Empire of Japan. . . . As Commander-in-Chief of the Army and Navy I have directed that all measures be taken for our defense. . . . I therefore ask that Congress declare that since the unprovoked and dastardly attack by Japan . . . a state of war has existed between the United States and the Japanese Empire."[8]
>
> —*PRESIDENT FRANKLIN D. ROOSEVELT, DECEMBER 8, 1941, IN HIS ADDRESS TO CONGRESS LEADING TO A DECLARATION OF WAR AGAINST JAPAN*

Roosevelt then wrote his famous speech—one that would forever be linked to the memory of Pearl Harbor. He simultaneously delivered it to Congress in person and the nation by radio on December 8. The Senate and House then voted almost

Franklin Roosevelt died in office on April 12, 1945,
before the end of World War II.

unanimously to declare war. Montana pacifist Jeannette
Rankin cast the only dissenting vote. At 4:00 p.m.,
Roosevelt signed the declaration. The United States had
entered World War II and was at war with Japan. ～

Chapter 4

Alien Enemies

The public and the media felt fear and anxiety in the days and weeks after Pearl Harbor. Japan was attacking and occupying other countries in Asia. Where was their next target going to be, people wondered—the West Coast of the United States mainland? If so, Japanese citizens lived in areas along the coast. Would they assist Japan in an invasion?

Immediately after Pearl Harbor, Roosevelt issued several presidential proclamations in reaction to that fear. They were aimed at alien enemies, which the government deemed to be individuals of German, Italian, and Japanese ancestry who were not US citizens but who were living in the United States. The government believed these aliens would show

The Japanese-American owner of this store put this sign up after the attack on Pearl Harbor.

an allegiance to their country of origin rather than the United States during the war. Proclamation 2525, aimed at Japanese aliens, was issued on the night of December 7, 1941. Proclamations 2526 and 2527, aimed at German aliens and Italian aliens respectively, were issued the next day. These proclamations assumed the United States would soon be at war with Germany and Italy. Indeed, war was declared only days later, on December 11.

> Whenever there is a declared war between the United States and any foreign nation or government, or any invasion or predatory incursion is perpetrated, attempted, or threatened against the territory of the United States by any foreign nation or government, and the President makes public proclamation of the event, all natives, citizens, denizens, or subjects of the hostile nation or government, being of the age of fourteen years and upward, who shall be within the United States and not actually naturalized, shall be liable to be apprehended, restrained, secured, and removed as alien enemies."[1]
>
> —US CODE AUTHORIZING PROCLAMATION 2525

After declaring that Japan invaded the United States, Proclamation 2525 went on to direct the conduct and activities of Japanese aliens over the age of 14 who lived within US borders. None would be allowed to fly in airplanes, and the government had the power to keep them out of designated areas such as power plants, dams, and weapons factories, among other regulations. The proclamation also stated that alien enemies could not possess firearms, weapons, ammunition, bombs, explosives, short-wave radios, transmitting sets, signal devices, cameras, papers with invisible writing, codes or ciphers, or plans or photographs detailing military information, such as military base locations or military equipment. It added that, "All such property found in the possession of any alien enemy in violation of the foregoing regulations shall be subject to seizure and forfeiture."[2]

Arrests

The Federal Bureau of Investigation (FBI) and local and military police began arresting and detaining Japanese aliens on the night of December 7. Prior to Pearl Harbor, the FBI had compiled a list, called the ABC list, of Japanese aliens targeted for arrest if war was declared with Japan. Those arrested were priests, community leaders, newspapermen, Japanese language teachers, and subscribers to publications the government believed were suspicious. There were 736 Japanese aliens arrested that night and smaller numbers of Italian and German aliens. Within four days, 1,370 Japanese aliens had

THE ABC LIST

By mid-1941, the names of more than 2,000 Japanese aliens were on the FBI's ABC list. The list divided suspect aliens into three categories. Group A included individuals considered known dangerous aliens, including fishers, Buddhist priests, and members of the Japanese Consulate. The individuals in Group B were thought to be potentially dangerous. People in Group C were thought to have pro-Japanese feelings or be involved in Japanese propaganda. They included martial arts instructors and Japanese language teachers.

been arrested.[3] This was legal according to the existing **statutes** that defined the government's wartime powers over alien enemies and the provisions of the presidential proclamations. Although foreign aliens enjoy many of the rights in the US Constitution, some legal protections are for US citizens only. For example, it is legal to deport aliens from the United States if they commit certain crimes.

statute—A law put into effect by the legislative branch of government.

Who's to Blame?

To assess the damage at Pearl Harbor, Secretary of the Navy Frank Knox visited the area on December 9. He was also investigating why the United States suffered such great losses. He needed to discover why Japan was able to succeed and why the navy was unprepared for the attack. The president and the public wanted answers. After his visit, Knox returned to the US mainland on December 15. He then told the press, "I think the most effective Fifth Column work of the entire war was done in Hawaii with the possible exception of Norway."[4]

The term *fifth column* refers to a network of spies working inside a country. In essence, Knox was laying blame on the ethnic Japanese in the United States for the Pearl Harbor attack. It was a damaging statement; however, the claim was not based on any evidence. On the contrary, Japanese Americans immediately worked to defend the islands during the attack. But because of Knox's position, his opinion was given a high degree of credibility. The press ran stories stating fifth-column activity was to blame for the attack, and the government did nothing to correct Knox's unproven statement. The idea quickly spread, and many soon believed Japanese

Americans were partly responsible for the attack on Pearl Harbor.

In an atmosphere of fear through which untruths were spreading, the general public and the government began believing that Japanese saboteurs and spies were living on the West Coast. They feared Japanese residents might be signaling from the shore to submarines in the ocean or somehow communicating with the Japanese military or government. Police raided the homes of thousands of Japanese aliens and removed cameras, flashlights, and items prohibited by Proclamation 2525 that could be used for signaling. In addition to the raids, Japanese assets in branches of Japanese banks in the United States were frozen, meaning individuals with accounts in those banks could no longer access their money.

Korematsu's Home

Korematsu's family home was raided a few days after Pearl Harbor. Because Korematsu's family home was next to a foundry, a place where metal is cast, it was put under watch by the military. He remembered,

> *They put spotlights on the whole nursery at night.*
> *And they had a guard standing right near our home,*

*right around the
fence there and
watching us.
One night . . .
I was standing
on the porch and
lit a cigarette
and the guard or
the person in the
foundry yelled out that I was signaling somebody.
Ridiculous, you know.*[5]

> " The police came down and confiscated all the flashlights and cameras. They didn't even have a search warrant or anything. They confiscated everything that they thought we might use for signaling."[6]
> —*KOREMATSU RECALLING THE POLICE RAID ON HIS HOME*

The Western Defense Command

To protect the West Coast, the US Army created the
Western Defense Command. Lieutenant General John
L. Dewitt, who had a history of prejudice against non-
Caucasian Americans, was in charge of the operation.
DeWitt, fearful of a second attack by the Japanese,
believed rumors about Japanese aliens and their possible
plans for sabotage. He thought the home raids were
necessary, and he pushed for more to be made without
issuing warrants. According to the 1983 US government
report *Personal Justice Denied,*

John L. DeWitt was deeply distrustful
of Japanese Americans.

*Dewitt's approach was routinely to believe almost
any threat to security or military control; not an
analyst or careful thinker who sought balanced
judgments of the risks before him, Dewitt did little
to calm the fears of West Coast people.[7]*

DeWitt believed the Japanese, both aliens and US
born, could not be trusted. As fear and anxiety grew on

the West Coast, so did DeWitt's mistrust of Japanese aliens and Japanese Americans. In January 1942, he told James Rowe, the US Assistant Attorney General,

> *I have little confidence that the enemy aliens are law abiding or loyal in any sense of the word. Some of them, yes; many, no. Particularly the Japanese, I have no confidence in their loyalty whatsoever. I am speaking now of the native born Japanese—117,000—and 42,000 in California alone.*[8]

DeWitt was not the only one who was beginning to believe all people of Japanese ethnicity were enemies of the United States. Politicians, the media, and the public were turning on Nisei and Issei. After decades of anti-Japanese sentiments, it did not seem unusual to mistrust

A SEGREGATED ARMY

Almost two years before Pearl Harbor, on December 5, 1939, DeWitt took command of the Fourth Army, which was headquartered in San Francisco. DeWitt's long service had been in a segregated army, before African Americans or Asians were allowed to serve alongside Caucasians. He had served in four tours in the Philippines, where he was undoubtedly exposed to prejudice against Asians— a prevalent attitude in the US Army at the time.

Japanese aliens and Japanese Americans. To many, the Japanese had always been unwelcome on the West Coast. Pearl Harbor provided further reason why they should not even be there—and many began publicly calling for their removal from the area.

"Japs"

Throughout January and early February of 1942, hysteria grew along the West Coast toward Japanese individuals, who were negatively called "Japs." *Los Angeles Times* newspaper headlines read, "[US] Representative Ford Wants All Coast Japs in Camps" and "American Japs Removal Urged."[9] The media often did not double-check accusations that Japanese aliens and Japanese Americans were spies and also rushed to print sensational headlines that fueled the hysteria. Some reporters not only failed to perform their journalistic obligation of objective investigation but also openly expressed their hatred for Japanese people. Columnist Henry McLemore wrote,

> *I am for immediate removal of every Japanese on the West Coast to a point deep in the interior. I don't mean a nice part of the interior either. Herd 'em up, pack 'em off and give 'em the inside room*

in the badlands. Let 'em be pinched, hurt, hungry and dead up against it. . . . Personally, I hate the Japanese. And that goes for all of them.[10]

The California legislature's Joint Immigration Committee sent a letter to California newspapers on January 2, calling for the removal of individuals of Japanese ancestry from coastal areas. The statement declared,

> *Those born in this country are American citizens by right of birth, but they are also Japanese citizens, liable . . . to be called to bear arms for their Emperor, either in front of, or behind, enemy lines.*[11]

This referred to the fact that Japanese Americans were considered to be Japanese citizens by the Japanese government, due to their parents' nationality. Some thought this automatic dual citizenship was proof of Japanese Americans' allegiance to Japan.

Soon Japanese Americans were fired from city positions. The Los Angeles County Board of Supervisors fired Nisei employees. It also adopted a **resolution**

resolution—A formal intention or opinion voted on by a lawmaking group or other body.

asking the federal government to remove all Japanese individuals from the West Coast. Sixteen other California counties joined in and passed their own formal resolutions. Individuals of Japanese ethnicity were barred from civil service positions and professional licenses to handle produce and run businesses were revoked. One county even demanded they stop farming.

West Coast politicians began voicing the need to evacuate all Japanese persons. Congressman Leland Ford of Los Angeles wrote to the secretaries of war and the navy, along with the FBI, on January 16, 1942. He stated that Californians were largely in favor of the evacuation of all Japanese people. Knowing that this was a complicated matter, especially when dealing with Nisei, who were US citizens, Ford wrote:

> *My suggestions . . . are as follows: . . . That all Japanese, whether citizens or not, be placed in inland concentration camps. As justification for this, I submit that if an American born Japanese, who is a citizen, is really patriotic and wishes to make his contribution to the safety and welfare of this country . . . that by permitting himself to be placed in a concentration camp, he would be*

JACL COOPERATION

Before Pearl Harbor, the JACL aided the FBI by adding names to its ABC list. In the months after Pearl Harbor, the organization was torn between proving its patriotism to the US government and standing up for the rights of Japanese Americans. Under its leadership at the time, the JACL chose to cooperate with the US government without question and advocate that position to the Japanese-American community. A JACL committee vowed in late 1941 to "inform on all individuals who appeared to be a danger to this country."[13]

making his sacrifice and he should be willing to do it if he is patriotic and is working for us.[12]

Groups such as the JACL agreed with this point of view, urging their members to prove their patriotism by preparing for an evacuation order and cooperating when the time came. Whether it was constitutional or not, the pressure was mounting for the federal government to take action against the Japanese. Not everyone agreed that internment was the right course to take. However, the recommendation of DeWitt and debates between government agencies would lead Roosevelt to make his historic decision about the fate of Japanese Americans during the war. ~

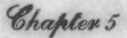

Chapter 5

The Decision to Exclude

Fear of a Japanese invasion and pressure from the public to remove Japanese people from the West Coast grew throughout February 1942. Although intelligence reports from the FBI and other sources concluded that there was no justifiable reason to suspect Japanese individuals in the United States of sabotage, the calls to exclude, or remove, them from the West Coast were loud and constant. On February 4, the army designated restricted areas along the coast and imposed a curfew for alien enemies of Japanese, Italian, and German descent, making it illegal for them to travel more than five miles (8 km) from their homes during the day. They also could not leave their homes from 9 p.m. to 6 a.m.

Within the US government, ways to deal with the "Japanese problem" were being hotly debated.[1] Members of the Justice Department were against the removal of Japanese individuals because of constitutional concerns, while the War Department, especially DeWitt, began to see it as a necessity. As the issue was debated in Washington DC, California state officials were under incredible pressure from the public. Many Caucasian Californians wanted all Japanese individuals to be excluded from the coast—but to do so would require a military justification to support the action.

DeWitt's Recommendation

To convince the Justice Department and the president that exclusion of people of Japanese descent from the West Coast was a military necessity, DeWitt submitted a recommendation to the secretary of war on February 14. This recommendation, "Evacuation of Japanese and Other Subversive Persons from the Pacific Coast," stated that certain areas in Washington, Oregon, and California were vital because of communication lines and industrial production, but they were open to air and naval attacks and sabotage. The letter further discussed the ethnic Japanese, their perceived untrustworthy personal nature due to their ethnicity, and their possible role in US sabotage:

> *In the war in which we are now engaged racial affinities are not severed by migration. The Japanese race is an enemy race and while many second and third generation Japanese born on United States soil, possessed of United States citizenship, have become "Americanized," the racial strains are undiluted. To conclude otherwise is to expect that children born of white parents on Japanese soil sever all racial affinity and become loyal Japanese*

DEWITT'S *FINAL REPORT*

In 1943, DeWitt completed his report, *Final Report: Japanese Evacuation from the West Coast, 1942*, on the War Department's justification for the internment of Nisei and Issei. The report listed several factors that supposedly made the evacuation a military necessity. Many of the factors had been proven by intelligence sources to be based on rumor, rather than facts. However, DeWitt presented them in his report as solid reasoning for exclusion. The report would later be examined and used by the Supreme Court in cases challenging aspects of the exclusion.

subjects, ready to fight and, if necessary, to die for
Japan in a war against the nation of their parents.[2]

DeWitt explained his belief that all persons
of Japanese ethnicity remained loyal only to Japan,
regardless of where they were born. His letter went on
to state that, if tested, even the Japanese born and raised
in the United States would turn against the nation and
assist Japan. With this belief, DeWitt wrote,

> *It, therefore, follows that along the vital Pacific*
> *Coast over 112,000 potential enemies, of Japanese*
> *extraction, are at large today. There are indications*
> *that these are organized and ready for concerted*
> *action at a favorable opportunity. The very fact that*
> *no sabotage has taken place to date is a disturbing*
> *and confirming indication that such action will*
> *be taken.[3]*

In sum, DeWitt felt the Japanese could not be trusted
because he believed their ethnicity automatically made
them enemies of the United States. If in fact no sabotage
had yet occurred, it meant sabotage was about to occur.
While the Justice Department was not convinced
exclusion was the right course to take, members of the
department knew the decision to exclude would soon be

COMMITTEE AGAINST EXCLUSION

The first official committee to examine if exclusion was the best course was the House Select Committee Investigating National Defense Migration, usually called the Tolan Committee. It began holding hearings on the West Coast in February and March 1942 to gather information about Japanese Americans and the exclusion on the West Coast. The committee eventually concluded that while there may have been some untrustworthy individuals, excluding all Japanese people from the area did not seem to be the best method to deal with the problem. The committee's report in May 1942 stated,

> The Nation must decide and Congress must gravely consider, as a matter of national policy, the extent to which citizenship, in and of itself, is a guaranty of equal rights and privileges during time of war.[4]

By the time the report came out, however, it was too late to stop the exclusion plans, which were already in motion.

made and they could not stop it. How to go about it was another question.

Executive Order 9066

The official decision for exclusion came ten weeks after the United States declared war on Japan. On February 19, 1942, Roosevelt signed Executive Order 9066. The order gave the secretary of war and certain military commanders the power to exclude any persons from designated areas in order to defend the nation against sabotage and espionage. It read,

> *Now, therefore, by virtue of the authority vested in me as President of the United States, and Commander in Chief of the Army and Navy, I hereby authorize and direct the Secretary of War, and the Military Commanders whom he may . . . designate, whenever he or any designated Commander deems such action necessary or desirable, to prescribe military areas in such places and of such extent as he or the appropriate Military Commander may determine, from which any or all persons may be excluded, and with respect to which, the right of any person to enter, remain in, or leave shall be subject to whatever restrictions the Secretary of War or the appropriate Military Commander may impose in his discretion.*[5]

The order, based on military justification, did not specify that it related directly to people of Japanese ancestry, although the president and government officials knew it was intended for use against that group of people. With the signing of this order, military commanders were

WESTERN DEFENSE COMMAND AND FOURTH ARMY
WARTIME CIVIL CONTROL ADMINISTRATION
Presidio of San Francisco, California
April 1, 1942

INSTRUCTIONS TO ALL PERSONS OF JAPANESE ANCESTRY

Living in the Following Area:

All that portion of the City and County of San Francisco, State of California, lying generally west of the north-south line established by Junipero Serra Boulevard, Worchester Avenue, and Nineteenth Avenue, and lying generally north of the east-west line established by California Street, to the intersection of Market Street, and thence on Market St to San Francisco Bay.

Once the government ordered the exclusion of people of Japanese heritage, notices such as this one were posted throughout the exclusion zones.

authorized to require Japanese Americans to move from the West Coast.

Now that exclusion was no longer under debate, the War Department and Western Defense Command were in charge of determining the logistical aspects of the exclusion. They had to choose which areas would be restricted. Most important, they had to figure out where to send 120,000 people of Japanese ancestry and how to get them there.

The First Steps

DeWitt's first approach to exclusion was voluntary. Issei and Nisei would have to leave restricted military

THE JACL'S OPINION

After Executive Order 9066 was issued, the JACL was invited to speak on behalf of Japanese Americans. Mike Masaoka, the National Secretary and Field Executive of the JACL, spoke before the Tolan Committee, which gathered information about exclusion for the House of Representatives. The JACL had decided to cooperate with the exclusion, and he was heavily involved with the decision. While he did not state the exclusion was wrong, Masaoka did say,

> At this hearing, we Americans of Japanese descent have been accused of being disloyal to these United States. As an American citizen, I resent these accusations and deny their validity.[6]

zones along the West Coast, but could move anywhere they wanted in interior areas of the United States. This approach failed and it did not make military sense. If Issei and Nisei were a real threat on the coast, why would they be less of a threat in interior states? Many dams, power lines, and other infrastructure were located there and could be damaged or spied upon. It was also impractical for Issei and Nisei. They would have had to voluntarily sell their businesses for unfair prices and move to unknown towns, where there was likely prejudice against people of Japanese ancestry.

Also, many had little access to funds because Japanese banks had been shut down and their assets frozen. Japanese-Americans' racial features did not allow them to physically blend into Caucasian or African-American society, so they could be easily pinpointed for hostile treatment. It did not make practical or financial sense to many in the Japanese community to move, so most stayed. The only effective method for the government's exclusion would be a mandatory move.

In order to make this effective, there needed to be a punishment for evading the exclusion. A bill was introduced in Congress in early March to make it a crime to evade the exclusion order, with mandatory imprisonment and a **misdemeanor** conviction as punishment. The bill passed and was signed into law as Public Law 503 on March 21, 1942.

Mandatory Removal

The restricted areas along the coast came under military control as designated military areas through

---

misdemeanor—A crime belonging to the less serious of the two categories of crime usually carrying a sentence of one year imprisonment or less.

Public Proclamation 1, which DeWitt issued on March 2, 1942. Military Area No. 1 was the land directly along the coast in California, Washington, and Oregon, and the southern part of Arizona. Military Area No. 2 was in the interior land of those states. It provided further restrictions on alien enemies (Japanese, German, and Italian) and all people of Japanese ancestry and extended the curfew. In a press release issued with the proclamation, DeWitt announced that Japanese people (both aliens and US citizens) would be moved from

GERMAN AND ITALIAN ALIENS

In 1942, there was a far larger population of German and Italian aliens in the United States than Japanese aliens. And unlike the Japanese population, their populations were not concentrated in a singular area. After the Pearl Harbor bombing, both German and Italian aliens were arrested if they were suspected of having Axis affiliations. By February 16, 1942, 1,393 Germans and 264 Italians had been detained. While the War Department considered extending the powers of Executive Order 9066 to German and Italian aliens on the West Coast, the plan did not go into effect. Detainees from the initial arrests were eventually sent to camps run by the Immigration and Naturalization Service. There they were given loyalty hearings and had good chances of being released. In contrast to the experience of Japanese Americans, US citizens of Italian and German descent were not interned during the war.

the military areas first, followed by the Germans and possibly Italians.

The army looked for sites where the Japanese evacuees could be sent to live, both temporary assembly center sites and long-term camp facilities called relocation centers. The assembly center locations were at racetracks and fairgrounds, where individuals would sleep in barracks, horse stalls, or other temporary lodgings. The more permanent relocation centers were later designated in areas of the Western states, internment camps surrounded by barbed wire and guard towers.

Handling the Removal

The War Department wanted to be free of the responsibility of the internment process, and it initiated the discussion about setting up a civilian agency to take over the enormous task. On March 11, 1942, the Wartime Civil Control Administration (WCCA) was created to handle the removal of the Japanese. The WCCA would supervise the first stage of the removal— moving people from the West Coast to the temporary assembly centers. To handle the second stage of the removal, the War Relocation Authority (WRA), a civilian agency, was established on March 18. The man chosen to head the WRA was Milton Eisenhower, the younger brother of Dwight Eisenhower, a military general who later became the thirty-fourth president of the United States. The WRA was designed to supervise evacuees once they left the assembly centers and to build and run the internment camps. Once the WRA was established, the War Department was set to begin its mass removal, and the official process of removal on the West Coast began. ∼

Chapter 6

Evading the Order

The process for mass removal began with the Civilian Exclusion Order and a notice of "Instructions to All Persons of Japanese Ancestry." The police posted both notices in public spots in the areas to be excluded, which were smaller exclusion zones carved out of the large Military Area No. 1. The first exclusion order was issued on March 24, 1942, for Bainbridge Island, near Seattle, Washington. The orders were kept a secret prior to their posting. Once posted, Issei and Nisei then had seven days before they would be removed from their homes. In the coming months, removal orders for many more exclusion zones followed.

Japanese Americans waiting to board relocation buses in San Francisco, April 6, 1942

The Civilian Exclusion Order stated that "all persons of Japanese ancestry, both alien and non-alien, be excluded" from that particular exclusion area.[1] Using the term *non-alien* instead of *citizen* is a noticeable distinction, covering up the reality that US citizens were being forced to leave. The area's boundaries were then described, including the street names that made up the boundaries of the area, and a map was included. The order went on to list a local meeting area, named a Civil Control Station, where "A responsible member of each family, and each individual living alone, in the [military area] will report between [specific hours]."[2] There, families would register for removal and be given a family number and identification tags. The order also stated the penalty for evading the order:

> *Any person subject to this order who fails to comply with any of its provisions of published instructions . . . or who is found in the [described] area after [the removal] . . . will be liable to the criminal penalties provided by Public Law No. 503 . . . and alien Japanese will be subject to immediate apprehension and internment.*[3]

The "Instructions to All Persons of Japanese Ancestry" notice explained a few other things Issei and Nisei needed to know. It listed the items they could bring with them to their new residence. Pets were not allowed and personal items could not be shipped. The instructions also stated that transportation would be provided—though where to was kept a secret.

The Reality of the Orders

With only seven days to settle their affairs, Japanese families lost money and possessions. Farms had to be abandoned with full crops growing. Property and businesses had to be quickly sold, and items put in storage or trusted to unreliable sources. What they could

WHAT THEY COULD BRING

The items that Issei and Nisei could bring to their new residences were:

"(a) Bedding and linens (no mattress) for each member of the family;

(b) Toilet articles for each member of the family;

(c) Extra clothing for each member of the family;

(d) Sufficient knives, forks, spoons, plates, bowls and cups for each member of the family;

(e) Essential personal effects for each member of the family."[4]

bring had to be labeled with their family's number. Then families boarded buses in public areas, where the whole town could see them, and were brought to assembly centers. The government set up these centers in West Coast communities to gather together the Japanese from the area before sending them to internment camps located further inland.

It was a frightening and humiliating experience—to be uprooted from a home, maybe the only home a Nisei had ever known, and then transported to an unknown place, where they would have to spend an undefined amount of time. Lives were completely interrupted and freedoms were lost. But the Japanese community complied, for the most part. Individuals did not want to be separated from their families. Some wanted to prove they were loyal Americans and believed that going without resistance would do so. Some protested and defied the internment, though—one being Fred Korematsu.

Korematsu's Evasion

Korematsu didn't purposely decide to defy Executive Order 9066 to prove it was unconstitutional. Mostly, he just didn't want to leave his girlfriend, who was a

ASSEMBLY CENTERS

From March 31, 1942, to August 7, 1942, approximately 92,000 people—70 percent of whom were US citizens—were evacuated to the 17 assembly centers.[5] Individuals did not know where they were going, and they were not sure what kind of clothing to bring for the climate where they would be interned. Most made the trip to the centers by bus or train, with armed guards patrolling them. In some trains, the windows were blacked out. When they arrived, Nisei and Issei first saw the barbed wire fences surrounding the centers, searchlights, and more armed guards. Once inside, individuals and families were grouped together in rooms. Bathrooms and showers did not have partitions—there was little to no privacy. The average stay in these centers was approximately 100 days.

Caucasian woman. He was young and in love, and he felt like a regular American. He wanted to go about his regular daily life, and he hadn't done anything wrong. Why should he have to leave?

On March 27, 1942, the area where Korematsu's family lived was included in a military order. No one of Japanese ancestry could leave the area, called Military Area No. 1. At the same time, Civilian Exclusion Order No. 34 was issued for the same area, directing Issei and Nisei to report to the area's Civilian Control Station, where they would be processed to go to the Tanforan

Assembly Center, a converted racetrack that held 8,000 people of Japanese descent.

Korematsu's family prepared to go, frantically packing up their belongings and deciding what to do about their nursery. Korematsu later recalled that time in their lives and how his parents felt:

> There was so much sadness . . . and so much worry because [they had] lived most of their lives at the nursery and in this country. . . . They obeyed the law and did what should be right; . . . they concentrate on raising their family, just the normal life. And to have this happen, it put them into shame. . . . When the evacuation notice came, they had to worry about what they were going to take and what was going to happen to the nursery. . . . They

TANFORAN ASSEMBLY CENTER

Twelve miles (19 km) south of San Francisco was the Tanforan Racetrack in San Bruno, California. This track became the site of the Tanforan Assembly Center. It contained 130 barracks for the evacuees to inhabit; most were located inside the track. The horse stables were also used as housing. Nisei and Issei tried to improve the center, planting gardens beside the barracks and building an aquatic park with a bridge, promenade, and islands.

would only give them a certain amount of time to do all that before they were pushed into camp.[6]

Korematsu decided he wasn't going with his family. He told them he was going to leave before the evacuation. As he recalled, they didn't try to stop him. His family was so busy and focused on getting ready to leave, they had no time to worry about Korematsu.

Korematsu rented a room in Oakland in the boardinghouse where his girlfriend lived. He went about a normal life and got a job welding at a company in Berkeley. To disguise his Japanese ancestry, Korematsu changed his name to Clyde Sarah and said he was of Spanish and Hawaiian descent. He altered his identification card to show his name change. He also had minor plastic surgery on his eyes to try to look less Japanese, something he later regretted doing and that did not really conceal his ethnicity.

Meanwhile, Korematsu's parents and brothers were sent to the Tanforan Assembly Center. They were to stay there until the permanent camps were built, which would be another five months. Korematsu bought a newspaper to learn more about the permanent camps. He later recalled,

I saw the pictures where the Japanese Americans were being marched into camp, and it sort of made me sick to my stomach. . . . I felt kind of lonely, like, what am I going to do now? I could see my parents going in and my brothers going into camp, and I'm not there. And I felt, sort of, all alone.[7]

Korematsu's Capture

On May 30, 1942, Korematsu planned to meet his girlfriend in San Leandro to go shopping. She was late, so Korematsu went into a store to buy something. When he came out, the police approached him and began questioning him. They asked for his identification and saw it had been altered. They listened to Korematsu's story about being Spanish and Hawaiian, but Korematsu could not speak Spanish. His story fell apart. The police took him to city hall and arrested him. It had been three weeks since his family was sent to Tanforan, and three weeks that he had been living in defiance of Civilian Exclusion Order No. 34. After the arrest, Korematsu never saw his girlfriend again.

Newspaper headlines reported Korematsu's arrest, stating "Two Bay Japs Evade Evacuation; Captured."[8] Of Korematsu, one *New York Times* article reported,

Residents of the Tanforan Assembly Center lining up outside the mess hall for a meal

"One tried to become Spaniard by plastic surgery."[9] Leaping to conclusions, another headline read, "Jap Spy Arrested in San Leandro."[10]

From the San Leandro jail, Korematsu was transferred to the Oakland jail. He stayed there for a week. Since he was charged with a **federal crime**, he was then transferred to the federal jail in San Francisco. ACLU lawyer Ernest Besig visited Korematsu at that jail. Besig had read the newspaper articles describing Korematsu's arrest and the arrests of two other Japanese-American men, Koji Kurokawa and John Ura. Besig met with the two other men: both declined his offer of legal representation and neither wanted to aim for a Supreme Court test case. But Korematsu was willing to take his case to the highest court. Korematsu knew his chances of winning were slim, but he was up for the fight. An FBI agent who had questioned him said Korematsu "stated that he believed the statute under which he was imprisoned was wrong . . . and that he intended to fight the case even before being approached by the Civil Liberties Union."[11] Korematsu, who just wanted

federal crime—A crime that breaks a US federal law rather than a state or local law.

CONFLICT IN THE ACLU

The national director of the ACLU, Roger Baldwin, did not want the ACLU to become involved with Japanese-American internment cases. Although he sympathized with the situation, he did not feel the test cases were strong enough. According to a later interview with Besig,

> [Roger Baldwin] had a lot of friends in Washington. . . . he knew the president, he knew the members of the cabinet; they were all his friends. I, I can't say that they induced him to take this position; I merely point out the fact that he was.[12]

The national ACLU, instead of forbidding the local chapters to take on these test cases, decided to limit what issues could be brought up in court, stating, "local committees are not free to sponsor cases in which the position is taken that the government has no constitutional right to remove citizens from military areas."[13] Local chapters could argue Japanese Americans had been singled out due to their ethnicity, though.

to continue living his life as an American, was now on a path to challenge the internment of Japanese Americans before the US Supreme Court. ~

Chapter 7

At Court
and in Camp

*K*orematsu was sent to the Tanforan Assembly
Center to await his trial, where he joined
his parents and brothers. He worried about what
other internees would think of his resistance and
arrest and hoped his family would not be treated
differently because of his actions. Because of this,
instead of staying with his family, he chose to have a
separate room. His room was one of the horse stalls
at the track, and he soon realized the conditions were
much worse than what he had experienced in jail.
Korematsu later recalled,

> *I opened the [stall] door; it had a gap of about*
> *six to eight inches from the ground, the dirt*

floor. And inside they just had a cot and a straw mattress in there. And there's gaping holes on all the walls; the wind . . . and the dust blew in there and everything. As I sat there, as I lied there to think it over, I guess I was there for about forty-five minutes and I said, boy, this is really a miserable place, no heat or anything. I mean, this was made for horses, not for human beings. I just wondered how in the world people lived in this for this long.[1]

At Tanforan, Korematsu found that he didn't have much support from the Japanese-American community. Many were afraid of what would happen if they resisted the military. They believed Korematsu's case would only make things worse. He was alone there—no one talked to or associated with him. But Korematsu kept his resolve. He later recalled thinking about his isolation at the center: "That didn't bug me because I'm an American and I wanted to fight it if I can. . . . I didn't like what was going on."[2]

Besig visited Tanforan and saw Korematsu while he awaited trial. During one visit, Korematsu handed Besig a note. In it, he wrote of the unfairness of the Japanese-American internment, how the assembly center was basically a jail, and how the entire situation went against

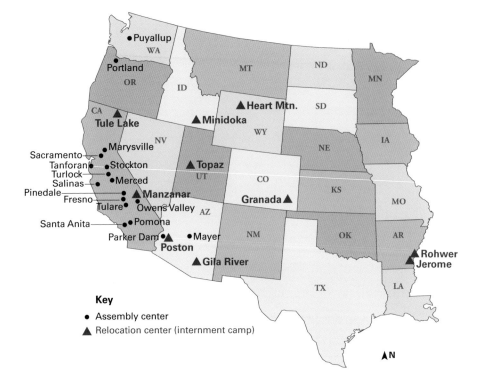

World War II Assembly Centers and Internment Camps

Key

- Assembly center
- ▲ Relocation center (internment camp)

the democratic way. He ended his note by saying his test case could help.

At Trial

On September 8, 1942, Korematsu's case was heard in the **United States District Court** for the Northern District of California. The case was known as *United States v. Korematsu* because the government was **prosecuting** Korematsu, the **defendant**. Judge Adolphus

St. Sure presided over the case. Since Besig was the director of the ACLU-NC and was not actively serving as a lawyer, Besig recruited Wayne Collins to represent Korematsu. Collins was a young San Francisco lawyer who had a small legal practice.

At the trial, Alfonso Zirpoli, the attorney representing the US government, proceeded first with his opening statement. He called one witness, FBI agent Oliver Mansfield, who had questioned Korematsu after

defendant—The person against whom legal action is brought.

prosecuting—Bringing legal action against someone.

United States District Court—A court that hears cases for federal crimes.

he was caught in San Leandro. Mansfield **testified** that Korematsu had admitted to forging his identification card, changing his name, and having plastic surgery. He said Korematsu said he stayed because "of friendly relationships with people there [and] that he considered himself to be an American and did not want to be evacuated . . ."[3] Zirpoli included Korematsu's forged identification card and birth certificate as **exhibits**, and then rested his case.

Since Zirpoli had proven Korematsu had purposely evaded the exclusion order, Collins attempted to introduce constitutional issues to the case. However, the judge denied his attempt. Korematsu then took the stand in his own defense. Collins knew the judge would find him guilty, but thought Korematsu's testimony might convince the judge to assign a lighter **sentence**. Korematsu told the judge about his background and schooling, assured him he had no attachment to Japanese culture, and stated: "As a citizen of the United States I am ready, willing, and able to bear arms for this country."[4]

Judge St. Sure was impressed with Korematsu's testimony but still found him guilty, convicting Korematsu of a federal offense. The judge did not impose a sentence, but he set **bail** at $2,500 and gave Korematsu five years of **probation**. At the time, a defendant could be put on probation without setting a sentence immediately. This decision made the situation more complicated later when the court of appeals took up the case. Next, as Korematsu recalled,

> To my surprise, Mr. Besig took out his checkbook and wrote [the bail amount] out, without hesitation, and gave it to the court. And he says, "Come on, Fred," he grabbed ahold of me, and we started walking out. . . . We finally got to the door, and I said, "Wow!" You know the sun was shining right in our face, and what a wonderful feeling to be free again, I thought.[5]

Usually once bail is set and paid, a defendant is allowed to go free until the case is appealed. Just outside the courthouse were military police, though. One pulled

bail—Money paid to allow a prisoner to be released temporarily.

exhibit—An item shown in court as evidence.

probation—The system of suspending a convicted offender's sentence and allowing the offender to remain free, dependent on good behavior.

sentence—A decision by a judge or court including the punishment for the person convicted.

testified—Declared something in court under oath.

a gun on Korematsu, saying he was not going to let Korematsu go. The judge was not sure what to do, so he raised Korematsu's bail to $5,000. Besig offered to cover this bail, but the military police said they had orders to apprehend Korematsu. Even though he was out on bail, Korematsu still had to report to his relocation center. The judge did not argue. The military police took Korematsu into custody and later returned him to Tanforan.

Appealing the Decision

If a defendant loses a case at trial but believes the judge made errors of law, he or she may seek to have the judgment overturned by an **appellate court**. Korematsu wanted to take an appeal to the United States Court of Appeals for the Ninth Circuit, an appellate court which includes California, with the possibility that the case would go from there to the US Supreme Court. The problem with appealing his case was that federal appellate courts usually only consider "final orders" of district courts. Because Judge St. Sure had not imposed a sentence on Korematsu, only a term of probation, it was not clear the case could be appealed right away.

At a hearing on December 23, 1942, Collins tried to convince Judge St. Sure to impose a sentence so the case could be appealed. But Judge St. Sure was unwilling to do so, stating, "I don't see any reason why I should make any change in my order to enable you to take this matter up on appeal."[6] The judge said he would consider the **motion**, but admitted that it would probably be denied. Until the judge made a decision, Korematsu's case would remain in limbo.

Life in Camp

In the meantime, Korematsu, along with the other internees at Tanforan, was moved to the Topaz War Relocation Center, an internment camp in Utah. The camp was located in a desert with harsh weather conditions. Winter temperatures fell below zero and summer temperatures reached into the nineties. When internees arrived, few of the barracks and none of the schools were finished being constructed. Some of the internees worked to complete the buildings. Workers in

appellate court—A court that can review and reverse the judgment of a lower court.

motion—A formal proposal to a court or judge asking for an order, ruling, or direction.

THE INTERNMENT CAMPS

Topaz was one of ten relocation centers in the United States. These large internment camps collected excluded Japanese and Japanese Americans from all over the West Coast and kept them imprisoned. They are sometimes called concentration camps. Internment camps were mostly located around the western part of the country in isolated areas. The Heart Mountain camp was near Cody, Wyoming, in a desert. The Minidoka camp, in Idaho, was also in a desert. Tule Lake and Manzanar were both camps in California, in areas with little vegetation. The Poston and Gila River camps were located in Arizona. The Granada camp was in Colorado. And the Jerome and Rohwer camps were in Arkansas.

the camps were paid for their labor. Barracks were simple structures without much insulation from the elements. They were constructed of pine planks covered by tar paper, with Sheetrock lining the inside walls. Army cots, mattresses, and blankets were the only furniture provided to internees in the rooms. Barbed wire and armed guards surrounded the camp, preventing the internees from escaping.

Korematsu and his family, six adults in total, shared two small rooms at the camp. He worked while he was there with a crew that built a hospital and performed other camp maintenance duties. It was miserable in

This shack at Manzanar internment camp in California was typical of internment camps around the country.

the camp. After a year and a half, Korematsu was able to leave Topaz to work in Salt Lake City, Utah. He left through a release program created by the government and intended only for proven loyal Japanese. After working in Utah, he moved to Detroit, Michigan, and studied to be a draftsman. Throughout this time, Besig kept in contact with Korematsu as his case progressed through its appeal.

The Court of Appeals

On February 19, 1943, the *Korematsu* case, along with two other cases challenging the internment, was heard before the United States Court of Appeals for the Ninth Circuit. The case was now known as *Korematsu v. The United States* because Korematsu was the **appellant**. Despite the fact that no sentence had been given in the *Korematsu* case, Collins still presented it to the court. The two other test cases were those of Minoru Yasui and Gordon Hirabayashi, represented by Earl Bernard and Frank Walters respectively. The cases were called *Yasui v. The United States* and *Hirabayashi v. The United States*.

While Collins—who pressed irrelevant issues and seemed angry—did not do a very good job in presenting Korematsu's appeal, Zirpoli also did not provide a convincing argument for the military necessity of the

appellant—A person appealing a case.

MINORU YASUI

Minoru Yasui was a trained army officer with a legal education who worked in the Japanese consular office. After a curfew was imposed for Japanese Americans on March 28, 1942, Yasui wanted to challenge it because of its unconstitutionality. He walked the streets of Portland, Oregon, that night, trying to get arrested. Yasui recalled of the night,

> I was getting tired walking around town, and I approached a policeman at eleven o'clock at night. I pulled out this order that said all persons of Japanese ancestry must be in their place of abode, and I pulled out my birth certificate and said "Look, I'm a person of Japanese ancestry, arrest me." And the policeman said, "Run along home, you'll get in trouble."[7]

Yasui finally walked into a police station and demanded to be arrested for curfew violation.

internment. Zirpoli argued that the internment was needed to keep Japanese Americans safe from people outside their community and that the inability of the government to determine who was loyal and disloyal meant all Japanese Americans needed to be interned. Edward Ennis, who worked for the Justice Department, made a statement along with Zirpoli that did not support his argument. Ennis admitted he knew of no

GORDON HIRABAYASHI

Gordon Hirabayashi was arrested on May 16, 1942, after presenting to the FBI a four-page letter outlining his reasons for refusing to register for evacuation. He was a student at the University of Washington in Seattle who was active in religious and social-action groups, and he was raised with pacifist beliefs. The internment went against all of his personal convictions. In his letter, Hirabayashi wrote:

This order . . . forces thousands of energetic, law-abiding individuals to exist in a miserable psychological and a horrible physical atmosphere. . . . If I were to register and cooperate under those circumstances, I would be giving helpless consent to the denial of practically all of the things which give me incentive to live.[8]

Japanese American who had been found to be a saboteur or a danger to military security.

Five weeks after the hearing, the court of appeals decided on an unusual action to take in the cases. Rather than provide a decision, on March 27, 1943, the court of appeals sent a **certified question** to the US Supreme Court asking it to resolve the legal questions raised.

The US Supreme Court is not required to answer a certified question, but it decided to hear the cases. **Chief Justice** Harlan Fiske Stone announced this move of the

THE ACLU AND THE *KOREMATSU* CASE

While the *Korematsu* case was stalled, the national ACLU was in conflict with the ACLU-NC. The national ACLU wanted to disassociate itself from the case and have Collins represent Korematsu as a private lawyer. Besig refused to back down at first, but then suggested that the national ACLU take over the case when it was to be heard by the Supreme Court. Besig realized the national ACLU's budget could better accommodate the costs of Korematsu's appeal. The national ACLU complied with Besig's suggestion and took over the case.

cases from the lower court to the US Supreme Court on April 5, 1943. Lawyers on both sides would have just six weeks to prepare for the arguments, scheduled to start on May 10, 1943. ~

certified question—A formal request by a lower court for the US Supreme Court to answer questions of federal law raised in the lower court.

chief justice—The presiding judge of the US Supreme Court.

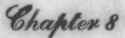

The US Supreme Court

ix weeks was a tight deadline to prepare for the US Supreme Court. The lawyers had assumed if the Supreme Court was going to hear the case, it might not happen for a year or more. They needed to quickly construct their **briefs** and prepare for their **oral arguments** before the judges. The questions the court of appeals posed to the court varied according to the case. For the *Hirabayashi* case, the question addressed the constitutionality of Public Law 503, the curfew, and the mass removal of Japanese Americans. In the *Yasui* case, US citizenship and its rights protected by the Constitution was the issue. In the *Korematsu* case, the question was not

92

yet about the removal and internment but whether the judges believed the case could be appealed, considering Korematsu had only received a probationary sentence.

The national ACLU no longer had faith in the legal skills of Collins, due to his poor performance in Korematsu's first trial and at the court of appeals. As Besig suggested, the national ACLU was now taking over, and its director, Roger Baldwin, wanted Collins off the case. He offered the case to A. L. Wirin, the lawyer for the ACLU chapter in Los Angeles, who seized the opportunity. Collins was not off the *Korematsu* case entirely, but Wirin would speak before the Supreme Court.

Solicitor General Charles Fahy was the head of the legal team representing the government, with Edward Ennis acting in an advisory role. The two differed in philosophy and personality. Ennis believed that Public Law 503 was unconstitutional and had disagreed with the War Department's arguments from the beginning. Fahy thought of the War Department as a legal client, which needed to be presented in the best light possible.

brief—A document that establishes the legal argument of a case.
oral argument—Spoken presentation of a legal case by a lawyer.

The government lawyers would not have much to do with the *Korematsu* case in its first round at the Supreme Court, since the question posed was about legal procedure. Instead they focused on the *Hirabayashi* and *Yasui* arguments. Fahy appointed John L. Burling, a Justice Department lawyer on Ennis's staff, to deliver the *Korematsu* argument.

Facing the lawyers were the **justices** of the Stone Court, named after Chief Justice Harlan Fiske Stone. Besides the chief justice, eight other Supreme Court

THE *RINGLE REPORT*

As the government lawyers prepared their brief for the *Hirabayashi* case, Edward Ennis discovered a report that had never been shown to the Justice Department. It was the *Ringle Report* from the Office of Naval Intelligence. Kenneth D. Ringle was the lieutenant commander of the office. Ennis alerted Solicitor General Charles Fahy to the report on April 30, 1943. The report was written on January 26, 1942, the month before Executive Order 9066 was signed. It stated that most, if not all, of the Japanese Americans who were a threat to the United States had been arrested during the ABC list roundup, meaning that the remaining Japanese Americans were of no threat to national security. Ennis wrote to Fahy, urging the report be submitted in the Supreme Court case. Fahy decided not to alert the Supreme Court to this report, though.

Chief Justice Stone, *front center*, and the Supreme Court justices who heard the *Korematsu* case

justices sit on the bench. The eight justices were: Hugo L. Black, William O. Douglas, Felix Frankfurter, Robert H. Jackson, Frank Murphy, Stanley Reed, Owen J. Roberts, and Wiley B. Rutledge. Stone called the justices his "wild horses," and the court was known for its frequent discord.[1] With such a reputation, no one could be sure how the court would decide the test cases.

justice—A member of the US Supreme Court.

The Supreme Court: Part One

On the afternoon of May 10, 1943, the nine Supreme Court justices emerged from behind a red velvet curtain in the court and took their seats at the bench. After swearing in eight lawyers to the Supreme Court bar and listening to the decisions of two previous cases before the court, the arguments for the three Japanese-American test cases began.

The *Hirabayashi* case was argued first by lawyers Frank Walters and Harold Evans. When arguing before the US Supreme Court, time is strictly limited. With this in mind, Walters began his argument. He had been given the task of reciting the facts of the case: the history of Executive Order 9066 and Public Law 503, the details of the curfew and evacuation orders, and the timeline of Hirabayashi's challenge of the curfew and evacuation. Justice Jackson asked Walters if DeWitt's orders were **bills of attainder**. In the US Constitution, this type of act is prohibited. Walters believed the orders were illegal bills of attainder, but Jackson continued questioning him

---

bill of attainder—A legislative act that singles out a person or group for punishment without a trial.

96

on this point and implied that military powers during war should not be questioned.

Evans next began his part of the argument, claiming that Public Law 503 granted power to DeWitt unlawfully and was too vaguely worded to provide DeWitt guidance in exercising those powers. To support his argument, Evans cited the decision in *Ex parte Milligan*, a Supreme Court case decided shortly after the US Civil War. The decision stated that a prisoner's ability to challenge his or her detainment could only be suspended for a short and finite time period. Evans moved on to challenge the scope of DeWitt's military orders, arguing that the West Coast did not represent a zone where invasion was imminent. He also noted that battle sites, such as Hawaii and other islands in the Pacific Ocean, were thousands of miles away from the coast. The justices challenged Evans and each other's opinions throughout the oral argument, questioning if the military was a better judge of whether US land might be invaded and arguing the relevancy of the *Milligan* decision to the case. The debate continued until Stone ended the arguments for the day. Evans did not have enough time to deliver all of his points.

THE *HIRABAYASHI* BRIEFS

The ACLU was not directly representing Hirabayashi, although he had their support. Instead, he had a legal team from Seattle, Washington. While the team prepared the *Hirabayashi* briefs, the ACLU tried to take control of the case. They found a more experienced lawyer to present the case to the court. When the *Hirabayashi* legal team decided to take the ACLU lawyer, they had to conform to the ACLU's orders about the internment case. They could not challenge the executive order, but they could challenge Public Law 503. However, two additional briefs were filed with the case—amici curiae briefs from the ACLU-NC and the JACL. Amici curiae briefs are submitted by a party not directly involved with a case that has an interest in the case and a perspective that may help the court decide. The ACLU-NC brief, written by Collins, attacked the executive order. Its submission in the case showed the Supreme Court justices the deep division in the ACLU at the time.

Filing an amicus curiae brief in the *Hirabayashi* case signaled a change in position for the JACL, which had previously supported the internment by promoting compliance. After meetings with Baldwin of the ACLU, the JACL decided to offer their support for the test cases. The brief, in part, argued that racism had been more of a motivator for the internment than any military threat.

The next day, May 11, lawyers Earl Bernard and Wirin presented the *Yasui* case to the court. Bernard stressed that Yasui's rights as a citizen were denied.

He focused on Yasui's loyalty to the United States despite his dual Japanese and American citizenship. Wirin spoke to the points of equal protection, DeWitt's racial prejudice, and undocumented reports of Japanese-Americans' espionage. He attacked DeWitt's judgment and the report of the Pearl Harbor commission, which he believed falsely claimed Hawaiians' involvement with the Pearl Harbor attack. While Justice Jackson admitted DeWitt might have made a mistake, he said the court needed to see much more evidence to determine if DeWitt had acted in bad faith. Justice Douglas added that even though some loyal Americans were evacuated, it did not affect the competence of DeWitt's military judgment. Evans disagreed and added as he ended his argument, "Neither color nor race has any military significance."[2]

Next the government had its chance to rebuke the *Hirabayashi* and *Yasui* arguments. Solicitor General Fahy took the podium, dismissed the allegations presented by Hirabayashi's and Yasui's lawyers, and delivered the main issue from the government's perspective—that due process is flexible, depending on the circumstances. In the circumstances of the time, the war powers of the government authorized actions that would not be tolerated in times of peace. Fahy defended Public Law 503, saying it was very clear in its essential purpose. He argued that Executive Order 9066 was incorporated into the law and that the law specified curfews and other restrictions as part of the military orders. Fahy then moved on to the government's main point, that a wartime emergency may justify certain restrictions on due process. Justice Jackson brought up the racial discrimination imposed by DeWitt's orders, stating,

> *We all agree that the Government may not say in peacetime that it is a crime for a descendant of an Irishman to do what would not be a crime if committed by a descendant of another national. The basis of discrimination is therefore in the war powers.*[3]

Fahy agreed that the curfew and removal of an ethnic group could not be done in peacetime, but disagreed that discrimination was involved with DeWitt's orders. Fahy instead argued that the orders were based on military necessity and described the perceived threat of espionage and sabotage on the West Coast. He argued that Japanese Americans had never assimilated into US culture, and the presence of Kibei (Japanese Americans who had been sent to Japan for their education) and

Japanese language schools made it seem reasonable to believe that if an invasion occurred, someone of Japanese descent on the West Coast might assist the Japanese. These were the reasons DeWitt recommended evacuation, Fahy contested, and they were not based on racial discrimination.

Wirin returned to the podium after Fahy was finished to present the *Korematsu* case. This argument was based on defining whether a probationary sentence could be appealed. This first had to be cleared up before Korematsu's case could be resolved by either the court of appeals or the Supreme Court. Burling, Wirin, and the justices discussed the technicalities of whether Korematsu's case could be appealed. Burling supported Wirin's claim that Judge St. Sure's refusal to assign a sentence to Korematsu should be treated as a final judgment, allowing the ruling to be appealed. With Burling's support, there was little doubt Korematsu's case

> "During time of war especially, it is not enough to say 'I am a citizen, and I have rights.' One must also say, 'I am a citizen, and I have obligations.'"[4]
>
> —*FAHY'S CLOSING STATEMENT*

would return to the Supreme Court. At the end of the day, the arguments had been presented, and it was time for the justices to deliberate.

On June 1, 1943, the justices delivered their decision on the *Korematsu* case. It was unanimous. The *Korematsu* case was appealable, and it would be sent back to the court of appeals for a decision on the exclusion order's legality. On June 21, Yasui's curfew violation conviction was upheld. Also on that day, the *Hirabayashi* decision was delivered. Instead of deciding whether the mass removal of Japanese Americans was constitutional, the justices focused on the legality of the curfew orders. They **sustained** his conviction, supporting the curfew orders and their legality. The mass removal issue would return to the Supreme Court, though. It would be examined in the *Korematsu* case, during its second round before the justices.

The Supreme Court: Part Two

By the time the decisions had been delivered in the *Hirabayashi* and *Yasui* cases, the public was beginning to debate whether the internment of Japanese Americans

sustain—To allow as valid in court.

was necessary. On the East Coast, newspaper articles questioned the internment, stating "Stigma by Ancestry" in one headline of the *Washington Post*.[5] On the West Coast, however, there was still support for the internment.

Korematsu's case headed back to the West Coast to be heard at the court of appeals. ACLU lawyers predicted it would soon be back before the Supreme Court, thinking it might be heard by June 1944. But, it would take longer than they thought. On December 2, 1943, the court of appeals upheld Korematsu's conviction, citing the Supreme Court ruling in the *Hirabayashi* case. The judges stated, "The government of the United

IN DETROIT

When *Korematsu* was being heard in the Supreme Court the second time, Korematsu himself was in Detroit, Michigan, working in a machine shop. He was still under the authority of the WRA, though. And as part of his federal conviction, Korematsu had to visit a probation officer each month. Besig kept in contact with him throughout the process of appeals. Korematsu remembered,

> [Besig] told me that [the case] was gonna be in the Supreme Court the next week, and he told me that, to cross my fingers hoping that something good would come out of it. And I was hoping that it would.[6]

States, in prosecuting a war, has power to do all that is necessary to the successful prosecution of a war."[7] They believed this was true even at the expense of certain rights of citizens. They added that the *Hirabayashi* decision overwhelmingly supported the evacuation, so there was no need to debate the point again.

To appeal this decision, Collins had to file a petition for a **writ of certiorari** within 30 days. Collins filed the petition and on March 27, 1944, the Supreme Court announced it would hear the *Korematsu* case. It was on the court schedule for the two weeks starting on April 17. However, the internment case of Mitsuye Endo had also been making its way through the legal system to the Supreme Court. To hear the two internment cases at the same time, *Korematsu* had to be delayed. On May 8, the Supreme Court issued the writ of certiorari, announcing it would hear both cases in October 1944.

The arguments began on October 11 with an unchanged lineup of justices. The chamber was filled with spectators anxious to hear the internment cases. Collins was back on the case and presenting the

writ of certiorari—An order from a higher court to a lower court calling for the record of a case for review.

Korematsu argument. Although the national ACLU was not impressed with Collins's skills, the regional ACLU wanted him on the case. With him was Charles Horsky, another ACLU lawyer. The two lawyers decided on a strategy of two parts: one part was to prove DeWitt's military necessity argument had no factual basis, and

MITSUYE ENDO

The case of Mitsuye Endo was heard along with Korematsu's case, but it was a separate case. Her case challenged the detention of loyal Americans and did not challenge the exclusion. After being dismissed from her job as a typist with the Department of Motor Vehicles in Sacramento, California, along with other people of Japanese descent, Endo was sent to the Tanforan Assembly Center. Endo's lawyer filed a habeas corpus petition on her behalf, asking the WRA to show reason why Endo should not be released from her internment. A habeas corpus petition asks that a court issue a command for a prisoner to be seen in a court on a certain date and time. The WRA offered to release Endo as long as she moved to an area away from the West Coast. This was done in part to avoid the case going to the Supreme Court, where the court might challenge the WRA's powers. Endo refused to abandon her case and remained interned for two more years. After her hearing at the Supreme Court, alongside Korematsu's case, the justices decided in favor of Endo, stating she was a loyal citizen and there were no grounds for her detainment.

the other part was to prove the exclusion orders led to detention regardless of an individual's loyalty to the United States. With this strategy, the legal team hoped to prove Korematsu's constitutional rights as a US citizen had been violated.

In his oral argument, Collins attacked DeWitt and his basis for the exclusion order, which was explained in DeWitt's *Final Report*. Justice Jackson asked Collins, "On what standard are we to say that he did not have any other facts?"[8] Collins answered that the Justice Department had admitted, in the first Supreme Court arguments, that DeWitt tended to base his military judgment on "tendencies and probabilities as evidenced by attitudes, opinions, and slight experience, rather than a conclusion based on ascertainable facts."[9]

Horsky's argument stressed the point that Congress, when approving Public Law 503, had supported only the removal of individuals from the West Coast, but not the detention of those individuals. By doing so, he hoped to show that the president had overstepped his executive powers. Horsky also attacked DeWitt's *Final Report*, pointing to a footnote in the government's brief that implied the Justice Department's objections to espionage allegations in the report. He pressed arguments about the

Charles Fahy was appointed solicitor general by Roosevelt.

report because Solicitor General Fahy had heavily relied on the report for the government's brief and argument.

When Fahy began his arguments, the justices pushed him to defend the detention issue. He responded that the detention was necessary as a preventive measure. He also quoted DeWitt's report throughout the outline of his argument, specifically citing a section that claimed radio transmissions had been intercepted and signal lights had been spotted along the coast. Fahy did this although he had read intelligence reports stating this information was false. Fahy concluded his argument on October 12, after which Endo's case was heard. With the arguments complete, the nine justices began their deliberations on October 16. It would be a heated debate—and not everyone would agree on the majority decision.

The Majority Opinion

The decisions in the *Korematsu* and *Endo* cases were announced on December 18, 1944. They came one day after the War Department announced that loyal Japanese Americans would be released from their internment on January 2, 1945. Those thought to be disloyal would remain interned.

In a 6–3 decision, Korematsu's federal conviction was upheld. Justice Black, known as a defender of civil rights, delivered the **majority opinion**. Black's opinion, rejecting Korematsu's contention that the exclusion order violated his constitutional rights, gave great weight to the military's wartime authority and the perceived military necessity as presented in DeWitt's report. At the beginning of the opinion, Black warned that the separation of a racial group should always be questioned:

> *It should be noted, to begin with, that all legal restrictions which curtail the civil rights of a single racial group are immediately suspect. That is not to say that all such restrictions are unconstitutional. It is to say that courts must subject them to the most rigid scrutiny. Pressing public necessity may sometimes justify the existence of such restrictions; racial antagonism never can.*[10]

The opinion went on to discuss the Supreme Court decision in the *Hirabayashi* case, stating:

> *We upheld the curfew order as an exercise of the power of the government to take steps necessary to prevent espionage and sabotage in an area threatened by Japanese attack. In the light of the principles we announced in the Hirabayashi case, we are unable to conclude that it was beyond the war power of Congress and the Executive to exclude*

majority opinion—An explanation of the reasoning behind the majority decision of the Supreme Court.

those of Japanese ancestry from the West Coast war area at the time they did.[11]

Justice Black continued by backing the military justification for the internment, stating:

We cannot reject as unfounded the judgment of the military authorities and of Congress that there were disloyal members of that population, whose number and strength could not be precisely and quickly ascertained. We cannot say that the war-making branches of the Government did not have ground for believing that in a critical hour such persons could not readily be isolated and separately dealt with, and constituted a menace to the national defense and safety, which demanded that prompt and adequate measures be taken to guard against it.[12]

66 To cast this case into outlines of racial prejudice, without reference to the real military dangers which were presented, merely confuses the issue."[13]
—*JUSTICE BLACK'S MAJORITY DECISION*

The justice went on to deny the decision to exclude individuals of Japanese ancestry was racially motivated. He added that calling the assembly and relocation centers "concentration camps" was unjustifiable, considering the ugly connotations that name carried in regard to the Jewish concentration camps in Europe. Justice Black affirmed that the exclusion order Korematsu evaded was within the government's legal rights and concluded,

> *Korematsu was not excluded from the Military Area because of hostility to him or his race. He was excluded because we are at war with the Japanese Empire, because the properly constituted military authorities feared an invasion of our West Coast and felt constrained to take proper security measures, because they decided that the military urgency of the situation demanded that all citizens of Japanese ancestry be segregated from the West Coast temporarily, and finally, because Congress, reposing its confidence in this time of war in our military leaders—as inevitably it must— determined that they should have the power to do just this.*[14]

Justice Frankfurter concurred with Justice Black's opinion and added his own, stating that he found "nothing in the Constitution which denies to Congress the power to enforce such a valid military order by making its violation an offense triable in the civil courts."[15] He added that making decisions of military necessity was for Congress and the president to decide, not the Supreme Court.

The majority dismissed concerns about racism. The Supreme Court backed the decisions made by Roosevelt and the War Department and DeWitt's argument of military necessity, thus supporting the mass removal of a single racial group.

The Dissents

Justices Roberts, Murphy, and Jackson opposed the majority decision and wrote stinging **dissents**. All believed racism was clearly involved in the case and that Korematsu's constitutional rights had been violated by the exclusion order.

Justice Roberts stated, "I dissent, because I think the indisputable facts exhibit a clear violation of Constitutional rights."[16] Unlike the *Hirabayashi* case, which involved a curfew violation, the *Korematsu* case involved imprisonment. It was:

dissent—An official written statement of a Supreme Court justice who disagrees with the majority decision.

[a] case of convicting a citizen as a punishment for not submitting to imprisonment in a concentration camp, based on his ancestry, and solely because of his ancestry, without evidence or inquiry concerning his loyalty and good disposition towards the United States.[17]

Justice Murphy stated in his dissent,

I dissent, therefore, from this legalization of racism. Racial discrimination in any form and in any degree has no justifiable part whatever in our democratic way of life. It is unattractive in any setting but it is utterly revolting among a free people who have embraced the principles set forth in the Constitution of the United States. All residents of this nation are kin in some way by blood or culture to a foreign land. Yet they are primarily and necessarily a part of the new and distinct civilization of the United States. They must, accordingly, be treated at all times as the heirs of the American experiment, and as entitled to all the rights and freedoms guaranteed by the Constitution.[18]

Justice Jackson's dissent asserted that Korematsu had not really committed a crime worthy of conviction, stating:

Korematsu was born on our soil, of parents born in Japan. The Constitution makes him a citizen of the United States by nativity and a citizen of California by residence. No claim is made that he is not loyal to this country. There is no suggestion that apart from the matter involved here he is not law-abiding and well disposed. Korematsu, however, has been convicted of an act not commonly a crime. It consists merely of being present in the state whereof he is a citizen, near the place where he was born, and where all his life he has lived. [19]

With these three dissents, it was made clear that the justices were deeply divided about the internment issue. But the majority decision stood, and the evacuation order was found to be constitutional. At the time, Korematsu and his lawyers could not predict the issue would be examined again in court. It would take nearly 40 years and an unexpected discovery by lawyer Peter Irons for that opportunity to arrive. ∼

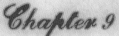

The *Coram Nobis* Case

*A*t the time of the *Korematsu* ruling, the country was divided about the internment. East Coast newspapers denounced the Supreme Court decision, calling it the "Legalization of Racism."[1] But support for the internment remained strong along the West Coast. The *Los Angeles Times* argued loyalty could never be determined and Japanese Americans should remain in the camps until the end of the war. The war was coming to a climax in Europe, where so many of the country's young men were fighting and dying to keep the Axis powers from gaining control.

The steps toward ending the internment had begun in early 1943. The government wanted the decision to end the internment to seem consistent with the original justification for internment. If not, it could make it seem as if the government had acted incorrectly. To do this, it was necessary to show there had been a change that proved the loyalty of Japanese Americans. The government decided to form an army regiment of loyal Japanese Americans who were previously not allowed to fight in the war. To determine loyalty, detainees were given a loyalty test. The questions were confusing, though, and the test angered detainees who had never shown disloyalty and had endured the harsh conditions of the camps. Although the test caused turmoil in the camps, the WRA and War Department deemed it a successful step toward ending the internment. Many detainees, including Korematsu, were given leave to depart the camps. The 442nd Infantry was formed in January 1943 of only Japanese Americans and went on to have many successes in battle in Europe during the war.

After these initial steps, the internment finally ended at the beginning of 1945. The War Department announced that the loyalty of the detainees being released had been proven. Throughout 1945, Japanese Americans left the camps. Many returned to the West Coast, including Korematsu's family. It was a traumatic experience to again be in a state of upheaval. Suicides occurred, and many were afraid they would return to a hostile public. They knew they would have to start their lives over from scratch.

Korematsu and His Family

Korematsu's family returned to their nursery in California. They found it in disrepair and began the hard task of rebuilding their business. Korematsu had continued with his life in Detroit, marrying his wife Kathryn. He moved with his wife back to California and had two children. World War II ended on

September 2, 1945, and the United States enjoyed peace once again. Korematsu's federal conviction followed him, however, blocking him from various employment opportunities. He later recalled,

> *When I first came back to California . . . I worked with my brother in real estate. And I wanted to be a real estate broker like he was. Well, in the application, they [asked] if I had a prison record, and therefore I knew it was useless to apply. . . . I knew they would turn me down.*[4]

Korematsu tried for other jobs, but many asked if he had a criminal record. He could find jobs only with smaller companies that did not offer retirement benefits. He said in 1983, "And that sort of affected my life. I'm still working, trying to work."[5]

Korematsu stopped talking about his Supreme Court case for years. He raised his family and became involved in social and church groups. But he still thought about his case, recalling,

> *And for forty years, I was wondering, I'd like to fight it because I said, am I an American or not? Can they do this again, send them away? So it bothered me.*[6]

During the decades following the decision, *Korematsu* was taught in law schools, and the Supreme Court judgment was widely condemned. Peter Irons, a lawyer who had learned about the *Korematsu* and *Hirabayashi* cases at Harvard Law School, took particular interest. He recalled, "I remember reading these cases and being struck with what seemed to me to be an obvious injustice . . ."[7]

Suppressed Information

In 1981, Irons began researching the Japanese-American internment cases for a book he was writing on the

PROCLAMATION 4417

Thirty-four years after it was issued, on February 19, 1976, Executive Order 9066 was terminated by the issuance of Proclamation 4417 by President Gerald Ford. It offered some consolation to Japanese Americans, admitting, "We now know what we should have known then—not only was that evacuation wrong, but Japanese-Americans were and are loyal Americans." It went on to state:

I call upon the American people to affirm with me this American Promise—that we have learned from the tragedy of that long-ago experience forever to treasure liberty and justice for each individual American, and resolve that this kind of action shall never again be repeated.[8]

subject of civil rights. As he searched through the Justice Department files related to the internment cases, it seemed to Irons that the files had not been touched since they were stored. Within the first five minutes of his research, Irons found a memo written by Edward Ennis to Solicitor General Fahy. It read,

> *We are in possession of information that shows that the War Department's report on the internment is a lie. And we have an ethical obligation not to tell a lie to the Supreme Court, and we must decide whether to correct that record.*[9]

Irons realized the Justice Department might have suppressed information in the *Korematsu* case. He also realized the memo could be an explosive piece of evidence against the government—evidence that could be used to reopen the internment cases. As he sifted through the files, Irons found more evidence of misconduct by the Justice Department and made copies to take with him. Irons believed the evidence he found might become the basis of ***coram nobis*** cases. A coram nobis petition is limited to cases where a fundamental

---

coram nobis—A petition that asks a court to reconsider a case that may have been unlawfully judged.

error or manifest injustice has occurred. It is a rarely used procedure. But Irons believed the records found could prove such an injustice had occurred. In the next few weeks, Irons decided to contact the defendants in the internment cases to see if they would like to reopen their cases using the coram nobis procedure.

After speaking with Hirabayashi and Yasui, Irons contacted Korematsu and told him he had found some records that might be interesting. Korematsu then invited Irons to his home. As they sat in his living room, Korematsu told Irons about his arrest and trial. He then carefully read the Justice Department records Irons had brought with him. When Korematsu was finished, he said "They did me a great wrong."[10] Along with Hirabayashi and Yasui, Korematsu decided to reopen his case.

Reopening Korematsu's Case

Irons put together a legal team to reopen the *Korematsu*, *Hirabayashi*, and *Yasui* cases. They were a group of young Japanese-American lawyers who included Dale Minami, Lorraine Bannai, Edward M. Chen, Dennis Hayashi, Karen Kai, Leigh-Ann Miyasato, Robert Rusky, Don Tamaki, and Eric Yamamoto.

Left to right: Hirabayashi, Yasui, and Korematsu asked the Supreme Court to reconsider its rulings on their cases.

On January 19, 1983, the lawyers filed a coram nobis petition on behalf of Korematsu in the Federal District Court for the Northern District of California. Included with the petition was proof that the government's intelligence agencies had concluded that Japanese Americans were loyal and had recommended against internment, that the government lawyers in *Korematsu* failed to provide this information during the case, and that an early draft of DeWitt's *Final Report* that did not support the government's argument in the case was revised and the original copies were burned.

The Coram Nobis Trial

Korematsu's trial was held on November 10, 1983, with Judge Marilyn Hall Patel presiding. The courtroom was packed with Japanese Americans who had also been in the internment camps during the war. Minami opened his argument, stating, "We are here today to seek a measure of the justice denied to Fred Korematsu and the Japanese-American community 40 years ago."[11] He acknowledged the government had already come a long way in saying Korematsu's conviction should be **vacated**. However, Minami disagreed with the government's

JUDGE MARILYN HALL PATEL

When Korematsu's lawyers heard Judge Marilyn Hall Patel was assigned to their case, they were very excited. Judge Patel had a reputation for being a sympathetic member of the district court toward civil rights and immigrant issues. She had worked for the Immigration and Naturalization Service in San Francisco and had supported progressive groups throughout her career. President Jimmy Carter appointed her to the federal bench in 1980.

position that there should be no acknowledgement of governmental error in the 1944 Supreme Court case. Minami stated,

> The government, however, is arguing that [the] findings, memorialized forever in a decision from the highest court of this land, now should be forgotten. It is arguing, in essence, that we should put the controversy behind us, that we should, in a sense, let old wounds heal.[12]

Minami also described the emotional and financial hardships suffered by Japanese Americans during the mass removal and internment and the evidence showing the government's suppression of vital information during Korematsu's Supreme Court trial. He said of the Japanese-American community: "They, too, have an interest in Fred's case, in Fred's vindication and to validate their own beliefs that they were not criminals in 1942."[13] Minami asked the judge to vacate Korematsu's federal conviction to achieve the justice he was denied by the US Supreme Court. Korematsu then made a statement:

vacated—Made legally void.

Your Honor, I still remember 40 years ago when I was handcuffed and arrested as a criminal here in San Francisco. . . . As an American citizen being put through this shame and embarrassment and also all Japanese-American citizens who were escorted to concentration camps, suffered the same embarrassment, we can never forget this incident as long as we live. . . . The horse stalls we stayed in were made for horses, not human beings.[14]

Korematsu continued, explaining how the US Supreme Court decision expressed to him that being a US citizen was not enough to prevent this kind of treatment. He said, "They say you have to look like [an American citizen], otherwise they say you can't tell a difference between a loyal and disloyal American."[15] He told the judge he believed that the decision in his case was wrong, adding, "As long as my record stands in federal court, any American citizen can be held in prison or concentration camps without a trial or a hearing."[16]

Victor Stone, representing the government, then presented his argument. He spoke about the Commission on Wartime Relocation and Internment of Civilians and its report, *Personal Justice Denied*, that he believed would affect Korematsu's conviction. He

COMMISSION ON WARTIME RELOCATION AND INTERNMENT OF CIVILIANS

In 1980, amid a movement by young Japanese Americans for compensation and redress, Congress appointed nine members to the Commission on Wartime Relocation and Internment of Civilians. Their job was to review the facts and circumstances that led to Executive Order 9066 and the internment of people of Japanese ancestry, and then recommend what remedial actions Congress should take. After a series of hearings in 1981, many including emotional testimonies from Japanese Americans, the commission released the report *Personal Justice Denied*.

also recounted the various efforts the government had made to compensate Japanese Americans. After Stone requested the petition be dismissed (relieving the government of accusations of wrongdoing), but that Korematsu's conviction be vacated, Judge Patel delivered an immediate response. She granted the petition, confirming the government had acted wrongly, and vacated Korematsu's federal conviction. The courtroom was speechless after Patel delivered her comments. Then, according to Irons, "Everybody got up and there was tremendous excitement. People were crying. Everybody was running up to congratulate Fred, pound him on the back."[17]

GOVERNMENT PARDON

During the coram nobis case, Korematsu was offered a government pardon. In essence, a pardon is a government's forgiveness for a person's crime. This would have removed Korematsu's conviction, but would not have cleared his name from the offense. Korematsu rejected the offer, since he did not believe he had committed a crime, saying, "I don't want a pardon. If anything, I should be pardoning the government."[19]

Patel's official opinion affirming this response was later released on April 19, 1984. It stated,

Korematsu *remains on the pages of our legal and political history. As a legal precedent, it is now recognized as having very limited application. As historical precedent it stands as a constant caution that in times of war or declared military necessity our institutions must be vigilant in protecting constitutional guarantees. It stands as a caution that in times of distress the shield of military necessity and national security must not be used to protect governmental actions from close scrutiny and accountability. It stands that in times of international hostility and antagonisms our institutions, legislative, executive, and judicial, must be prepared to protect all citizens from the petty fears and prejudices that are so easily aroused.*[18]

While Patel's decision did not change the US Supreme Court decision, it did give public recognition that the government had done an injustice to the Japanese-American community. The win was a moment Korematsu and the entire Japanese-American community had been waiting years to witness. ∿

Chapter 10

The Legacy of the *Korematsu* Decision

The decision to vacate Korematsu's conviction was one step toward addressing the injustices committed against Japanese Americans. Another step was the report issued in 1983 by the Commission on Wartime Relocation and Internment of Civilians. In its report *Personal Justice Denied*, the commission concluded there had been no military justification for Executive Order 9066. In the years after the report was released, Korematsu became an outspoken advocate for the redress of Japanese Americans.

President Bill Clinton presented Korematsu with the Presidential Medal of Freedom in 1998.

On August 10, 1988, President Ronald Reagan signed the Civil Liberties Act of 1988 and acknowledged that the internment was unjust. This act provided a formal apology sent in a letter and $20,000 in financial compensation to each survivor of the internment.[1] It had been 40 years since the internment ended, though, and many internees had died. The act could not overturn the Supreme Court decision, however.

Korematsu continued to work for civil rights, and on January 15, 1998, President Bill Clinton awarded him the Presidential Medal of Freedom. The medal is the highest civilian honor given by the government. During his speech, President Clinton said, "In the long history

REDRESS FOR JAPANESE AMERICANS

In 1990, surviving internees received $20,000 checks and government apology letters signed by President George H. W. Bush. The letters stated:

A monetary sum and words alone cannot restore lost years or erase painful memories; neither can they fully convey our Nation's resolve to rectify injustice and to uphold the rights of individuals. We can never fully right the wrongs of the past. But we can take a clear stand for justice and recognize that serious injustices were done to Japanese Americans during World War II.[2]

of our country's constant search for justice, some names of ordinary citizens stand for millions of souls. Plessy, Brown, Parks . . . to that distinguished list, today we add the name of Fred Korematsu."[3]

After many years of advocating for civil justice and the rights of all Americans, Korematsu died on March 30, 2005, at the age of 86. His name had become famous for his landmark case, which continues to teach Americans lessons about their government and the obligations and rights of US citizens.

REMEMBERING KOREMATSU

Korematsu's legacy lives on in many ways. In 2001, the documentary *Of Civil Wrongs and Rights* was released, telling the story of Korematsu's life and his court cases. In 2005 and 2006, two elementary schools were named after Korematsu: the Fred T. Korematsu Elementary School at Mace Ranch in Davis, California, and the Fred T. Korematsu Discovery Academy in Oakland, California. In 2009, the Fred T. Korematsu Institute for Civil Rights and Education was launched in San Francisco, California. This institute works to advance civil and human rights through education, activism, and leadership development. Its Web site contains civil rights lessons for all grades. On September 23, 2010, the state of California officially designated January 30, Korematsu's birthday, as the Fred Korematsu Day of Civil Liberties and the Constitution.

Repeating *Korematsu*?

After the tragedy of the September 11, 2001, terrorist attacks in New York City, Washington DC, and Pennsylvania, the treatment of Arab Americans and Muslims echoed the experiences of Japanese Americans 60 years earlier. The tragedy was instantly compared to the attack on Pearl Harbor, and the government's response to 9/11 was compared to the response of the Roosevelt administration. Hate crimes against Arab Americans and Muslims increased, and the public thought Arab Americans should be watched. Some believed immigrants from countries with terrorist affiliations should be interned. The police questioned individuals on the strength of little evidence other than ethnicity. Hundreds were arrested or detained. By November 2001, 1,100 people, mostly men of Middle Eastern descent, were in law enforcement custody.[4] Many did not know for months why they had been arrested.

The *Korematsu* case was being talked about again, as well. But not in defense of Arab Americans' rights; rather, it was discussed in support of the expansion of government powers. Some conservative commentators argued that the internment had been justified. They

The United States has detained prisoners
from the conflicts in Iraq and Afghanistan at the detention
camp in Guantanamo Bay, Cuba.

used the Supreme Court's decision in *Korematsu* as a
legal authority for the government's infringement on
civil rights when dealing with national security issues.
In 2003, Congressman Howard Coble stated that he
thought the internment of Japanese Americans had
been the right thing to do during World War II, adding,
"Some were probably intent on doing harm to us, just

as some of these Arab Americans are probably intent on doing harm to us."[5]

Different cases arose after 9/11, challenging the treatment of Arab Americans and aliens in US prisons. Korematsu continued to speak out. In 2003, in a case before the Supreme Court, *Rasul v. Bush*, he filed an amicus brief on behalf of Muslims imprisoned at the Guantanamo Bay prison in Cuba. He joined them in challenging the government's right to hold foreign nationals in the Guantanamo prison for an indefinite period without receiving a trial. In 2004, the Supreme Court ruled that detainees should have access to US courts to challenge their detention.

In 2004, Korematsu filed a similar brief supporting a Muslim man who had not been given a trial and who was imprisoned in a US military jail. This was the case of *Rumsfeld v. Padilla*, which drew parallels between Korematsu's and Padilla's detainment. In his brief, Korematsu warned the government not to make the mistakes of the past. However, the case was dismissed on a technicality.

Examining the *Korematsu* Decision

Despite Korematsu's vindication through his coram nobis case, the Supreme Court decision stands. While it could technically be used as a precedent, it is highly unlikely. As was concluded in *Personal Justice Denied*, "Today the decision in *Korematsu* lies overruled in the court of history."[6] Some wonder: Could an ethnic group's internment ever happen again? While it is unlikely that a mass internment could ever occur again in the United States, Korematsu's case teaches that the wartime expansion of powers may or may not be justified but should always be examined, and the results of those powers may have lasting, negative effects on society.

> " There are Arab Americans today who are going through what Japanese Americans experienced years ago, and we can't let that happen again. I met someone years ago who had never heard of the roundup of Japanese Americans. It's been sixty years since this [arrest] happened, and it's happening again, and that's why I continue to talk about what happened to me."[7]
>
> —*KOREMATSU, IN THE DOCUMENTARY OF CIVIL WRONGS AND RIGHTS*

The main legal issue that Korematsu's case raises is equal treatment of US citizens. The Fifth Amendment requires the federal government to grant due process of law to all persons, and due process requires equal treatment. The *Korematsu* decision showed that during war, expanded government powers may revoke those rights and not all citizens may enjoy the same freedoms. And with the Japanese-American internment, the civil liberties of one ethnic group were denied due to those expanded powers.

Today, the *Korematsu* decision is commonly condemned as a civil rights disaster. The Japanese-American mass removal and internment is viewed as an

APOLOGY FROM THE SOLICITOR GENERAL

On May 20, 2011, US Solicitor General Neal Katyal made an official apology for the Japanese-American internment. In his apology, Katyal acknowledged the decision of Solicitor General Fahy to suppress key information in Korematsu's case. Katyal wrote,

Today, our Office takes this history as an important reminder that the 'special credence' the Solicitor General enjoys before the Supreme Court requires great responsibility and a duty of absolute candor in our representations to the Court. Only then can we fulfill our responsibility to defend the United States and its Constitution, and to protect the rights of all Americans.[8]

exaggerated and unfounded response by the government during a time of war, the results of which ignored the importance of civil liberties for an ethnic group. The court decision remains as an example of the legislative branch failing to uphold constitutional rights in deference to wartime executive powers. As learned from *Korematsu*, it is every citizen's right to question laws that suppress his or her civil liberties. Doing so may prevent the injustices suffered by Japanese Americans from ever happening again. ～

TIMELINE OF EVENTS AND RULINGS

1919

September 30 — Fred T. Korematsu is born in San Francisco, California.

1941

December 7 — The surprise attack on Pearl Harbor decimates US naval forces stationed at the base.

December 8 — The United States declares war against Japan.

December 15 — US Secretary of the Navy Frank Knox tells the press fifth column work aided the Pearl Harbor attack.

1942

February 19 — President Franklin D. Roosevelt signs Executive Order 9066.

March 27 — Civilian Exclusion Order No. 34 is issued for the area where Korematsu's family lives.

May 30 — Korematsu is captured and jailed for his evasion of the Civilian Exclusion Order.

September 8 — Korematsu's case is tried in the US District Court for the Northern District of California.

1943

February 19 — The court of appeals hears the *Korematsu*, *Hirabayashi*, and *Yasui* cases.

March 27 — The court of appeals does not decide on the internment cases, but instead invokes a certified question to the US Supreme Court.

April 5 — The US Supreme Court decides to hear the *Hirabayashi*, *Yasui*, and *Korematsu* cases.

1943	June 1	The US Supreme Court rules that the *Korematsu* case is appealable, despite its lack of a sentence.
	December 2	The court of appeals upholds Korematsu's conviction.
1944	October 11–12	The US Supreme Court hears the *Korematsu* and *Endo* cases.
	December 17	The War Department states that loyal Japanese Americans will be released from internment.
	December 18	The US Supreme Court delivers its decision in the *Korematsu* case, upholding Korematsu's conviction.
1945	**September 2**	World War II ends.
1948	July 2	The Japanese American Evacuation Claims Act is signed into law. It offers to compensate internees.
1976	**February 19**	President Gerald Ford issues Proclamation 4417, terminating Executive Order 9066.
1983	**January 19**	A coram nobis petition is filed on behalf of Korematsu.
	November 10	Korematsu's coram nobis trial is held. His federal conviction is vacated.
	December	The Commission on Wartime Relocation issues its report *Personal Justice Denied*.
1988	**August 10**	President Ronald Reagan signs the Civil Liberties Act of 1988.
2005	March 30	Korematsu dies at the age of 86.

GLOSSARY

alien enemy

    A foreign-born resident of a country who is considered to be an enemy of that country due to his or her nationality.

ancestry

    A person's family or ethnic descent.

exclusion

    The act of preventing or restricting the entrance of a person or group of people from a particular area.

internee

    A person who has been confined within the limits of a country or place especially during a war.

internment

    The confinement of a person or group of people for political or military reasons.

mass removal

    The removal of a large group of people from a specific area.

military justification

    A reason for an action that is deemed necessary by the military in order to maintain national security.

pacifist

    A person who is strongly opposed to conflict and war.

presidential proclamation

An order issued by the president directed at individuals and not legally binding unless Congress has passed a law authorizing the order or the order is part of the president's constitutional powers.

propaganda

Ideas, actions, or messages spread to further a cause.

redress

Compensation for a wrong or loss.

saboteur

A person who is destructive or carries out obstructive actions in order to impede a country's war effort.

segregation

The separation of a race, class, or ethnic group.

BRIEFS

Petitioner

Fred T. Korematsu

Respondent

The United States

Date of Ruling

December 18, 1944

Summary of Impacts

After Korematsu evaded an exclusion order for all people of Japanese ancestry, he was captured and arrested. After being convicted of a federal crime, Korematsu decided to join with the American Civil Liberties Union to appeal his conviction and serve as a US Supreme Court test case. His case was heard before the US Supreme Court in 1944, where the justices heavily relied on DeWitt's *Final Report* to prove military justification for the mass removal and internment of people of Japanese ancestry. It was later discovered that the US Justice Department had intelligence information that proved the *Final Report* was not factually based, and therefore did not prove military justification, but this information was withheld from the Supreme Court justices during the case.

The court's 6–3 ruling upheld Korematsu's conviction. Justice Hugo L. Black delivered the majority decision, which supported the military justification for the mass removal and internment of people of Japanese ancestry, denying that racism was involved. Three justices opposed the majority decision and wrote stinging dissents: Justices Roberts, Murphy, and Jackson. All believed racism was clearly involved in the case and that Korematsu's constitutional rights had been violated by the exclusion order. Although the government later admitted the mass removal and internment had been a grave injustice, the US Supreme Court ruling still stands. While it could technically be used as a precedent, it is highly unlikely. As was concluded in *Personal Justice Denied*, "Today the decision in *Korematsu* lies overruled in the court of history."

Quote

"Korematsu was born on our soil, of parents born in Japan. The Constitution makes him a citizen of the United States by nativity and a citizen of California by residence. No claim is made that he is not loyal to this country. There is no suggestion that apart from the matter involved here he is not law-abiding and well disposed. Korematsu, however, has been convicted of an act not commonly a crime. It consists merely of being present in the state whereof he is a citizen, near the place where he was born, and where all his life he has lived."

—*Justice Robert H. Jackson, in his dissent to the majority decision*

ADDITIONAL RESOURCES

Selected Bibliography

Bannai, Lorraine K. "Taking the Stand: The Lessons of Three Men Who Took the Japanese American Internment to Court." *Seattle Journal for Social Justice* 4.1 (2005). *Korematsu Institute.* "The Coram Nobis Cases." Web. 22 Apr. 2011.

Irons, Peter. *Justice at War.* New York: Oxford UP, 1983. Print.

United States. Commission on Wartime Relocation and Internment of Civilians. *Personal Justice Denied.* Washington, DC: The Commission, 1983. *National Archives and Records Administration.* PDF file. Web. 8 June 2011.

Further Readings

Chander, Anupam, and Madhavi Sunder. *Fred Korematsu: All American Hero.* Durham, NC: Carolina Academic, 2011. Print.

Elinson, Elaine, and Stan Yogi. *Wherever There's a Fight: How Runaway Slaves, Suffragettes, Immigrants, Strikers, and Poets Shaped Civil Liberties in California.* Berkeley, CA: Heyday, 2011. Print.

Web Links

To learn more about *Korematsu v. The United States*, visit ABDO Publishing Company online at **www.abdopublishing.com**. Web sites about *Korematsu* are featured on our Book Links page. These links are routinely monitored and updated to provide the most current information available.

Places to Visit

Japanese American Museum of San Jose
535 North Fifth Street, San Jose, CA 95112
408-294-3138
http://www.jamsj.org
This museum's permanent exhibit *World War II: Assembly Centers and Internment Camps* features photographs, drawings, handicrafts, and artifacts from an internment camp.

Japanese American National Museum
369 East First Street, Los Angeles, CA 90012
213-625-0414
http://www.janm.org
This museum is the largest dedicated to the history of Americans of Japanese ancestry. Its permanent collection includes diaries, photographs, and paintings created by Japanese Americans during their internment at various camps.

Minidoka National Historic Site
Jerome County, ID
208-933-4127
http://www.nps.gov/miin/index.htm
Now part of the National Park Service, this site is the home of the Minidoka Relocation Center for Japanese Americans. Visitors can see the entry station, waiting room, and rock garden. They can walk along paths through the camp and read interpretive signs about the internment.

SOURCE NOTES

Chapter 1. An Unexpected Visitor

1. Lorraine K. Bannai. "Taking the Stand: The Lessons of Three Men Who Took the Japanese American Internment to Court." *Seattle Journal for Social Justice* 4.1 (2005): 10. Korematsu Institute. "The Coram Nobis Cases." Web. 22 Apr. 2011.

2. Fred Korematsu. "No Place in the Union." *Tracked in America*. Tracked in America, n. d. Web. Audio transcript. 30 Apr. 2011.

3. Fred Korematsu. "Internment." *Tracked in America*. Tracked in America, n. d. Web. Audio transcript. 30 Apr. 2011.

4. Ibid.

5. Fred Korematsu. "Fred Korematsu—Kathryn Korematsu Interview Segment 4." *archive.densho.org*. Densho Digital Archive, 14 May 1996. Web. 30 Apr. 2011.

6. Henry David Thoreau. "Civil Disobedience—Part 2 of 3." *The Thoreau Reader*. Web. 1 May 2011.

Chapter 2. The Japanese in the United States

1. "A Century of Lawmaking for a New Nation: U.S. Congressional Documents and Debates, 1774–1875." *Library of Congress*. Library of Congress, 1 Mar. 1790. Web. 13 May 2011.

2. United States. Commission on Wartime Relocation and Internment of Civilians. *Personal Justice Denied*. Washington, DC: The Commission, 1983. Chapter 1, p. 30. *National Archives and Records Administration*. PDF file. 13 May 2011.

3. Ibid. Chapter 1, p. 32.

4. Ibid. Chapter 1, p. 35.

5. "TAKAO OZAWA v. US, 260 U.S. 178 (1922)." *FindLaw*. FindLaw, n.d. Web. 17 May 2011.

6. Lorraine K. Bannai. "Taking the Stand: The Lessons of Three Men Who Took the Japanese American Internment to Court." *Seattle Journal for Social Justice* 4.1 (2005): 10. Korematsu Institute. "The Coram Nobis Cases." Web. 22 Apr. 2011.

7. Ibid.

Chapter 3. The Attack on Pearl Harbor

1. Lorraine K. Bannai. "Taking the Stand: The Lessons of Three Men Who Took the Japanese American Internment to Court." *Seattle*

Journal for Social Justice 4.1 (2005): 10. Korematsu Institute. "The Coram Nobis Cases." Web. 22 Apr. 2011.

2. Fred Korematsu. "Fred Korematsu—Interview Segment 1." *archive.densho.org*. Densho Digital Archive, 14 May 1996. Web. 17 May 2011.

3. Andy Stephens. "Paradise Lost: The Legacy of the 11th Bomb Group." *Air Force Print News Today*. US Air Force, 8 Dec. 2011. Web. 9 Jan. 2012.

4. "Remembering Pearl Harbor: Multimedia Map and Time Line." *National Geographic*. National Geographic, n. d. Web. 18 May 2011.

5. United States. Commission on Wartime Relocation and Internment of Civilians. *Personal Justice Denied*. Washington, DC: The Commission, 1983. Chapter 2, p. 47. *National Archives and Records Administration*. PDF file. 13 May 2011.

6. Lorraine K. Bannai. "Taking the Stand: The Lessons of Three Men Who Took the Japanese American Internment to Court." *Seattle Journal for Social Justice* 4.1 (2005): 10. Korematsu Institute. "The Coram Nobis Cases." Web. 22 Apr. 2011.

7. "FDR and Pearl Harbor." *Franklin D. Roosevelt Presidential Library and Museum*. Franklin D. Roosevelt Presidential Library and Museum, n. d. PDF file. 18 May 2011. 16–17.

8. "Transcript of Joint Address to Congress Leading to a Declaration of War Against Japan (1941)." *www.ourdocuments.gov*. www.ourdocuments.gov, n. d. Web. 18 May 2011.

Chapter 4. Alien Enemies

1. "United States Proclamations Regarding Alien Enemies." *The American Journal of International Law* 36.4, Supplement: Official Documents (Oct. 1942): 236–243. *JSTOR*. Web. 18 May 2011.

2. Ibid.

3. Peter Irons. *Justice at War*. New York: Oxford UP, 1983. Print. 19.

4. United States. Commission on Wartime Relocation and Internment of Civilians. *Personal Justice Denied*. Washington, DC: The Commission, 1983. *National Archives and Records Administration*. PDF file. Chapter 2, p. 55.

5. Lorraine K. Bannai. "Taking the Stand: The Lessons of Three Men Who Took the Japanese American Internment to Court." *Seattle Journal for Social Justice* 4.1 (2005): 10. Korematsu Institute. "The Coram Nobis Cases." Web. 22 Apr. 2011.

6. Ibid.

7. United States. Commission on Wartime Relocation and Internment of Civilians. *Personal Justice Denied.* Washington, DC: The Commission, 1983. Chapter 2, p. 64. *National Archives and Records Administration.* PDF file. 13 May 2011.

8. Ibid. Chapter 2, p. 65.

9. "Determining the Facts, Reading 1: Fear." *Teaching with Historic Places Lesson Plans.* National Park Service, n. d. Web. 23 May 2011.

10. United States. Commission on Wartime Relocation and Internment of Civilians. *Personal Justice Denied.* Washington, DC: The Commission, 1983. Chapter 2, p. 72. *National Archives and Records Administration.* PDF file. 13 May 2011.

11. Ibid. Chapter 2, p. 68.

12. Ibid. Chapter 2, p. 70.

13. Peter Irons. *Justice at War.* New York: Oxford UP, 1983. Print. 77–79.

Chapter 5. The Decision to Exclude

1. United States. Commission on Wartime Relocation and Internment of Civilians. *Personal Justice Denied.* Washington, DC: The Commission, 1983. Chapter 2, p. 72. *National Archives and Records Administration.* PDF file. 13 May 2011.

2. Ibid. Chapter 2, p. 82.

3. Ibid.

4. Ibid. Chapter 2, p. 86–87.

5. "Transcript of Executive Order 9066: Resulting in the Relocation of Japanese (1942)." *100 Milestone Documents.* ourdocuments.gov, 19 Feb. 1942. Web. 25 May 2011.

6. *Hearings Before the Committee Investigating National Defense Migration*, Part 29, 21 and 23 Feb. 1942. Washington, DC: United States Government Printing Office, 1942. 11229–11232. *archive.org.* Web. 25 May 2011.

Chapter 6. Evading the Order

1. United States. Commission on Wartime Relocation and Internment of Civilians. *Personal Justice Denied*. Washington, DC: The Commission, 1983. Chapter 3, Figure A: An Exclusion Order. *National Archives and Records Administration*. PDF file. 13 May 2011.

2. Ibid.

3. Ibid.

4. Ibid. Chapter 3, Figure C: Instructions to Evacuees.

5. Ibid. Chapter 5, p. 135.

6. Lorraine K. Bannai. "Taking the Stand: The Lessons of Three Men Who Took the Japanese American Internment to Court." *Seattle Journal for Social Justice* 4.1 (2005): 8. Korematsu Institute. "The Coram Nobis Cases." Web. 22 Apr. 2011.

7. Ibid. 9.

8. Ibid. 10.

9. "3 JAPANESE DEFY CURBS: Army Says One Tried to Become 'Spaniard' by Plastic Surgery." *New York Times*. New York Times, 13 Jun. 1942. Web. 22 Apr. 2011.

10. Fred Korematsu. "Do we really need to relearn the lessons of Japanese American internment?" *SFGate.com*. San Francisco Chronicle, 16 Sept. 2004. Web. 28 May 2011.

11. Peter Irons. *Justice at War*. New York: Oxford UP, 1983. Print. 98.

12. Ernest Besig. "Ernest Besig Interview Segment 7." *archive. densho.org*. Densho Digital Archive, 14 May 1996. Web. 31 May 2011.

13. Peter Irons. *Justice at War*. New York: Oxford UP, 1983. Print. 130.

Chapter 7. At Court and in Camp

1. Lorraine K. Bannai. "Taking the Stand: The Lessons of Three Men Who Took the Japanese American Internment to Court." *Seattle Journal for Social Justice* 4.1 (2005): 10. Korematsu Institute. "The Coram Nobis Cases." Web. 22 Apr. 2011.

2. Ibid. 12.

3. Peter Irons. *Justice at War*. New York: Oxford UP, 1983. Print. 152.

4. Ibid. 152–153.

5. Lorraine K. Bannai. "Taking the Stand: The Lessons of Three Men Who Took the Japanese American Internment to Court." *Seattle Journal for Social Justice* 4.1 (2005): 10. Korematsu Institute. "The Coram Nobis Cases." Web. 22 Apr. 2011.

6. Peter Irons. *Justice at War*. New York: Oxford UP, 1983. Print. 162.

7. Ibid. 84.

8. Ibid. 88.

Chapter 8. The US Supreme Court

1. Peter Charles Hoffer, Williamjames Hull Hoffer, and H.E.H. Hull. *The Supreme Court: An Essential History*. Lawrence, KS: University Press of Kansas, 2007. 282.

2. Peter Irons. *Justice at War*. New York: Oxford UP, 1983. Print. 222–223.

3. Ibid. 225.

4. Ibid. 226.

5. Ibid. 251.

6. Fred Korematsu. "Fred Korematsu - Kathryn Korematsu Interview Segment 5." *archive.densho.org*. Densho Digital Archive, 14 May 1996. Web. 31 May 2011.

7. Peter Irons. *Justice at War*. New York: Oxford University Press, 1983. Print. 258.

8. Ibid. 314.

9. Ibid.

10. "TOYOSABURO KOREMATSU v. UNITED STATES, 323 U.S. 214 (1944)." *FindLaw*. FindLaw, n. d. Web. 5 June 2011.

11. Ibid.

12. Ibid.

13. Ibid.

14. Ibid.

15. Ibid.

16. Ibid.

17. Ibid.

18. Ibid.

19. Ibid.

20. Lorraine K. Bannai. "Taking the Stand: The Lessons of Three Men Who Took the Japanese American Internment to Court." *Seattle Journal for Social Justice* 4.1 (2005): 10. Korematsu Institute. "The Coram Nobis Cases." Web. 22 Apr. 2011.

Chapter 9. The Coram Nobis Case

1. Peter Irons. *Justice at War*. New York: Oxford University Press, 1983. Print. 346.

2. "Check for Compensation and Reparations for the Evacuation, Relocation, and Internment." *National Archives*. National Archives, n. d. Web. 6 June 2011.

3. "JA History." *Japanese American Citizens League*. Japanese American Citizens League, 2002. 10. PDF file. 27 May 2011.

4. Fred Korematsu. "Fred Korematsu Interview Segment 8." *archive.densho.org*. Densho Digital Archive, 15 Nov. 1983. Web. 6 June 2011.

5. Ibid.

6. Lorraine K. Bannai. "Taking the Stand: The Lessons of Three Men Who Took the Japanese American Internment to Court." *Seattle Journal for Social Justice* 4.1 (2005): 10. Korematsu Institute. "The Coram Nobis Cases." Web. 22 Apr. 2011.

7. Peter Irons. "Peter Irons Interview II Segment 6." *archive. densho.org*. Densho Digital Archive, 27 Oct. 2000. Web. 6 June 2011.

8. "President Gerald R. Ford's Proclamation 4417, Confirming the Termination of the Executive Order Authorizing Japanese-American Internment During World War II." *Ford Library Museum*. Ford Library Museum, n. d. Web. 6 June 2011.

9. Peter Irons. "Peter Irons Interview II Segment 12." *archive. densho.org*. Densho Digital Archive, 27 Oct. 2000. Web. 6 June 2011.

10. Peter Irons. *Justice at War*. New York: Oxford UP, 1983. Print. 367.

11. Peter Irons, ed. *Justice Delayed: The Record of the Japanese American Internment Cases*. Middletown, CT: Wesleyan UP, 1989. Print. 214.

12. Ibid. 217.

13. Ibid. 218.

14. Ibid. 220.

15. Ibid. 220.

16. Ibid. 220–221.

17. Peter Irons. "Peter Irons Interview II Segment 21." *archive. densho.org*. Densho Digital Archive, 27 Oct. 2000. Web. 6 June 2011.

18. Peter Irons, ed. *Justice Delayed: The Record of the Japanese American Internment Cases*. Middletown, CT: Wesleyan UP, 1989. 243.

19. Eric Yamamoto and May Lee. "Excerpts from A BRIEF BIOGRAPHY: FRED KOREMATSU." *Asian American Bar Association*. Asian American Bar Association, n. d. Web. 6 June 2011.

Chapter 10. The Legacy of the *Korematsu* Decision

1. Lorraine K. Bannai. "Taking the Stand: The Lessons of Three Men Who Took the Japanese American Internment to Court." *Seattle Journal for Social Justice* 4.1 (2005): 10. Korematsu Institute. "The Coram Nobis Cases." Web. 22 Apr. 2011.

2. "Official Apology from the United States Government." *Discover Nikkei*. Discover Nikkei, n. d. Web. 8 June 2011.

3. Akil Vohra. "Honoring Fred Korematsu." The White House: Office of Public Engagement. The White House: Office of Public Engagement, 1 Feb. 2011. Web. 8 June 2011.

4. Lorraine K. Bannai. "Taking the Stand: The Lessons of Three Men Who Took the Japanese American Internment to Court." *Seattle Journal for Social Justice* 4.1 (2005): 10. Korematsu Institute. "The Coram Nobis Cases." Web. 22 Apr. 2011.

5. Ibid. 36.

6. United States. Commission on Wartime Relocation and Internment of Civilians. *Personal Justice Denied*. Washington, DC: The Commission, 1983. Chapter 8, p. 238. *National Archives and Records Administration*. PDF file. 13 May 2011.

7. Lorraine K. Bannai. "Taking the Stand: The Lessons of Three Men Who Took the Japanese American Internment to Court." *Seattle Journal for Social Justice* 4.1 (2005): 10. Korematsu Institute. "The Coram Nobis Cases." Web. 22 Apr. 2011.

8. Neal Kaytal. "Confession of Error: The Solicitor General's Mistakes During the Japanese-American Internment Cases." *The White House: Initiative on Asian Americans and Pacific Islanders*. The White House: Initiative on Asian Americans and Pacific Islanders, 20 May 2011. Web. 8 June 2011.

INDEX

About the Author

Karen Latchana Kenney is an author and editor from Minneapolis, Minnesota. She has written more than 60 educational books, with topics ranging from life in the Middle Ages to the issues of illegal immigration and domestic violence. Her books have received positive reviews in *Booklist*, *Library Media Connection*, and *School Library Journal*.

About the Content Consultant

Richard D. Friedman earned a BA and JD from Harvard University and a DPhil from Oxford University. He is the Alene and Allan F. Smith Professor of Law at University of Michigan Law School and an expert on Supreme Court history.